Lee at Fredericksburg

Duty Most Sublime

The Life of Robert E. Lee
As Told Through the "Carter Letters"

by
William Franklin Chaney

GATEWAY PRESS, INC.
Baltimore, MD   1996

Please direct all correspondence and book orders to:
The 1861 Company
5728 South East Crain Hwy.
Suite 1861
Upper Marlboro, MD 20772

Library of Congress Catalog Card Number 96-77584
ISBN 0-9653685-0-5

Typesetting by The LetterEdge

Published for the author by
Gateway Press, Inc.
1001 N. Calvert Street
Baltimore, MD 21202

Printed in the United States of America

TABLE OF CONTENTS

ILLUSTRATIONS

ACKNOWLEDGEMENTS

The one individual whose work on this project has been indispensable is my editor, Tom Nugent. He led me by the hand from a rough, early manuscript to the finished book, and his enthusiasm for the task never waned.

I received a great deal of assistance from the library staff at Washington and Lee University, which I first visited in 1994. General Lee loved both the university and Lexington, and it was easy to see why. C. Vaughn Stanley, Special Collections Librarian at the James G. Leyburn Library and his assistant Lisa McCown, were the embodiment of Southern kindness. They generously shared the General's letters, and provided endless information and assistance. General Lee would be very proud of his people at Washington and Lee!

Henry M. Hall and Carter C. Shepherd got me started on the research that led to the "Goodwood" and Robert E. Lee connection. Rosalie Eugenia Oster kindly spoke with me for hours and permitted me to tape our conversation about the Carters and the Lees. Her graciousness gave me an insight into the ladies the Carter girls must have been. Annette C. Lennig, a granddaughter of Annette Carter, to whom General Lee wrote many of the enclosed letters, was also of great assistance and a joy to speak to. Mrs. Lennig passed away in January, 1996.

Photographs, letters and much useful information were provided by Martha Forbes Boone, Alice Carter Bowie, Oden Bowie, Eleanor Mae Forbes Carrico, Robert A. Crawley, Louise Rede Davis, Josephine Addison Gamble, Peggy George, Marie Forbes Gessner, Carter Hall, Margaret Hall, John Mitchell, Lynn and Eugene Bowie Roberts, Jr., Annette Roberts Slowenski, Sarah Carter Staples, Anne Lee Davis Sullivan, Robert Lee George Williams, and Jan and William Woodyear, Jr.

The Tudor Place Foundation and the Riversdale Historical Society, Inc., provided me with helpful information about Tudor Place and Riversdale.

Ann Munro Wood painted the frontispiece and did the sketches in the book. She is an artist of immense talent and a pleasure to work with.

Thanks also to the Greenbrier Hotel in West Virginia, where Lee and the Carters frequently visited, for some invaluable information.

Jack Frazer of Annapolis helped tremendously in gathering information and locating others who had pertinent materials. Equally helpful were Margaret Kieckhefer, Dennis McNew and Jim Higgins of the Library of Congress.

The staff of the Maryland Archives in Annapolis—and especially Nancy Bramucci—were very cooperative. The Archives remain one of Maryland's best-kept secrets.

The Enoch Pratt Free Library in Baltimore very kindly granted permission to reprint materials, as did the Maryland Historical Society in Baltimore, the Duke University Library, and the University of Virginia Library. The Virginia Historical Society in Richmond kindly gave their permission to reprint some Lee letters, and Ann Marie Price was especially helpful in this regard.

Elliott Owens accompanied me to many battlefields, and to Washington and Lee and Stratford Hall. Lyle Russell of the Prince George's County Register of Wills office was quite helpful, and Craig Reinhardt, Carol Jackson, Donna Bunn and Cindy Kumbar all assisted me with my computer work.

Thanks also to Karen Lowe and Dorothy Lowman, who helped me in many different ways with this project.

Finally, I would like to thank my family for putting up with me and listening to me talking constantly about the Carters, the Calverts and of course, General Robert E. Lee.

—William Franklin Chaney, 1996

INTRODUCTION

The family of Lee ... has more men of merit in it than any other family.

—John Adams

This book is about the life of Robert Edward Lee, the greatest man to have emerged from a family of great men. I have tried to show General Lee's life in a version that would emphasize the highlights of his remarkable story, while at the same time exploring his relationship with his cousin from Southern Maryland, Charles Henry Carter, through letters from Lee to Carter—and also through letters from Lee to two of Carter's daughters, Annette and Ella.

Robert E. Lee married Mary Randolph Custis; Charles Henry Carter married Rosalie Eugenia Calvert. Both women were descendants of the Calvert family of Maryland. Mary Custis and Eugenia Calvert were cousins who grew up in the high Southern society of the early 19th Century. When they were single, Lee's brother, Carter Lee, wrote a poem about the beauty of these two girls.

Nelly Custis (related to both girls and granddaughter of Martha Washington) wrote in one of her letters that she wished her son would marry "either Mary Custis or Eugenia Calvert." [1]

Lee and Carter were related through both the Lee and Carter families. And their marriages to cousins made their families doubly related—so that it was quite natural for them to maintain a close relationship throughout their lives. Robert and Mary Lee's three sons and four daughters and the Carters' six daughters and one son would visit each other frequently at "Arlington," the Lee home, and "Goodwood," the Carter home.

Along with telling the dramatic story of these two important families, I wanted to describe the political climate before and during the War for Southern Independence in Maryland, where Charles Henry Carter resided.

The history of Maryland during this era seems quite paradoxical: most Americans think of Maryland as a "Union" state. And it is true that northern and western Maryland were mostly pro-Northern. Still, there's no doubt that the majority of those living in the Old Line State supported the South.

Maryland's Governor Thomas Hicks, a pro-Union man, said in a speech in January of 1861, while refusing to call the legislature into special session (because he knew the legislators would vote for Secession): "That Maryland is a conservative Southern State, all know who know anything of her people or her history."

Only Hicks' treachery and Abraham Lincoln's disregard for the Constituiton kept Maryland in the Union.

I have tried to show these different aspects of Maryland's unique history, along with Lee's relationship with his Maryland cousins. But the heart of the book is the story of Robert E. Lee's amazing life. Most Americans think of this man only as a great military genius. But he was much more. He was an educator, a kind and gentle man, a good family man and a devout Christian.

He was a man of impeccable character and integrity—a man who defined his own nature perfectly when he uttered the famous line:

"The most sublime word in the English language is 'duty.'"

Children of Robert Edward Lee and Mary Anna Randolph Custis Lee **"ARLINGTON"**	Children of Charles Henry Carter and Rosalie Eugenia Calvert Carter **"GOODWOOD"**
George Washington Custis Lee (1832–1913)	Rosalie Eugenia Carter Hall (1832–1875)
Mary Custis Lee (1835–1918)	Alice Carter Bowie (1833–1905)
William Henry Fitzhugh Lee (1837–1891)	Bernard Moore Carter (1834–1912)
Anne Carter Lee (1839–1862)	Ella Carter George (1836–1894)
Eleanor Agnes Lee (1841–1873)	Mildred Carter (1839–1920)
Robert Edward Lee, Jr. (1843–1914)	Annette Carter Brogden (1840–1917)
Mildred Childe Lee (1846–1905)	Mary Randolph Carter Bier (1843–1871)

—————————— • ——————————

Arlington — Built by Mrs. Lee's father, George Washington Parke Custis, in 1802. Located in northern Virginia on a hill overlooking Washington, D.C. Robert and Mary Lee lived there until the War began.

Cedar Grove — Home of Julia Calvert Stuart, sister of Rosalie Eugenia Carter and cousin of Mary Custis Lee. Bridesmaid in Lee wedding. Located in the northern neck of Virginia.

Goodwood — Home of the Carters. Built by George Calvert in the 1790's. Located in Queen Anne, Prince George's County, Maryland.

Ravensworth — Home of the Fitzhughs, cousins of the Lees and Carters. Located in Virginia.

Shirley — Ancestral home of the Carters, located in Virginia.

Stratford — Ancestral home of the Lees, located in Virginia.

White House — A Lee home where George and Martha Washington were married, located in Virginia.

CHAPTER ONE

Robert E. Lee
and his Maryland Cousins

I proposed to [daughter] Annie, the only one who could leave home, that we should ride down to Goodwood, which we reached about dark & found [Cousins] Charles, Mildred and Annette. They sent the next morning early for Eugenia and Alice, who came over for the day with some of their children. I had a very pleasant time, as it was the first holiday I had taken since my return from [U.S. Army duty in] Texas.

Everything was looking very beautiful. The house had been painted & done up. The trees had grown very much, & the flowers were very beautiful & pretty. ...[2]

—Robert E. Lee in a letter to his son Rooney, describing happy days at "Goodwood," two years before the outbreak of the War for Southern Independence: May 30, 1859.

It was as close to heaven as the earthbound can ever get.

The scene: an immense, three-winged brick mansion, looming majestically from the top of a bright green hill.

Executed in the Federal architectural style that was so popular in the America of the 19th Century, the soaring "Goodwood" plantation-house shines like a mighty beacon in the late afternoon light.

Move in a bit closer, and you can watch the playful spring breeze looping among the tossing branches of oak and locust and wild cherry. Watch that brown squirrel—there he goes! darting from his perch in the tallest oak, spooked and chattering furiously, as two people on horseback go cantering along beneath the tree. ...

Underneath the stately old oak at the foot of the hill that cradles "Goodwood," the two riders slowly pass.

The lead figure is obviously a distinguished military officer—his easy grace in the saddle tells you that. Slender of build and neatly groomed, he's surely a cavalryman, and probably a graduate of West Point. Beside him rides a graceful young woman on a chestnut roan, probably his daughter; she's smiling happily as they drift toward the great house that awaits them on the crest of the hill.

These two are enjoying the spring breeze; they're taking their time. Laughing and pointing, they can't get enough of the local sights, the smells, the comical burlesque of two black crows yapping at each furiously on a nearby branch.

Goodwood

They've arrived.

The year is 1859; the month is May.

For Robert E. Lee and his daughter Annie, this visit to the "Maryland Cousins"—the family of Charles Henry Carter and his seven lively offspring—is to be a too-brief interlude, a moment of peace and contentment, a tranquil hour filled with small, ordinary pleasures before the great storm that is coming breaks around them, and destroys such tranquility forever.

For the Lees, one of Virginia's great ruling families, these periodic visits to Goodwood, near Upper Marlborough, Maryland, provide a restful, refreshing oppportunity to get to know the "Maryland side" of their kinfolk: the great swarm of cousins, nieces, nephews, uncles, aunts and in-laws who entered the world of the Lees with the marriage of Charles Henry Carter (twice-related to Robert E. Lee) and Rosalie Eugenia Calvert (the daughter of George Calvert and a direct descendant of Lord Baltimore, the founder of the Old Line State of Maryland).

Watch, now, as the two horses reach the great, slant-roofed barn on the outskirts of Goodwood ... as the servants hurry out to take the bridles and lead the famished steeds off toward food and rest ... as Robert E. Lee and his daughter Annie stride toward the front doors of the great mansion that is Goodwood.

How splendid, how satisfying, to have been young and eager and alive in that Maryland Maytime of 1859!

But did they sense—as the great, oaken doors of Goodwood came groaning open to receive them—how quickly that time was running out?

Did they hear the faint, distant howling of the approaching storm ... as the afternoon's last light fell like burnished gold upon the elegant grass of this ancestral home?

Robert E. Lee's noble presence and gentle, kindly manner were sustained by religious faith and an exalted character.

—Winston Churchill

Robert E. Lee was the greatest American military tactician of his era ... a natural-born genius of the battlefield whose astonishing gift for command would almost singlehandedly rescue the South from her inevitable defeat in the War for Southern Independence.

But Lee's prowess as a tactician did not detract from his other great strength as a West Point-trained officer: his amazing knack for leadership, a personal magnetism so unerringly powerful that tens of thousands of ordinary foot-soldiers were willing to "plunge into the jaws of hell" at the first command from the silver-bearded general in the Confederate gray.

A descendant of the aristocratic Lee and Carter families of Virginia, Robert E. Lee was a classic example of the social ideal known as "noblesse oblige"—the principle that requires "honorable, generous and responsible behavior" from all citizens of high birth.

A lovingly supportive father, a loyal husband and a fervent Christian who abjured the use of profanity throughout his life, Lee observed the very highest standards in all of his conduct. While leading the heroic Army of Northern Virginia through some of the bloodiest campaigns in the history of modern warfare, for example, he steadfastly refused to mimic the strategy of the Union generals: Lee would not make war on the civilian populace.

Later, after the war had been lost (1865) and Lee had been named the President of Washington College in Lexington, Virginia, he sought to live up to the highest standards of "Christian forgiveness" ... by insisting that the embittered South must put the ghastly war behind it, and accept its tragic fate as a working-out of "Divine Providence." Intent on passing the stern tests of "noblisse oblige" to the end, the weary general spent his last years in Lexington in a continuing search for ways to help the shattered South heal from the double wound of miltary defeat and humiliating Reconstruction.

By now, of course, Lee's permanent image as a beloved American who became a symbol of "duty and honor" is enshrined in the pantheon of national heroes, and his place in history is secure. The great Union General, Ulysses S. Grant—Lee's major adversary during the final chapter of the war—admitted as much, himself, only a year or so after Appomattox, when he described Lee thus: "There was not a man in the Confederacy whose influence with the whole people was as great as his."

Born at Stratford Hall (near Montross), Virginia, on Jan. 19, 1807, Lee was the scion of Virginia's leading family. While one of his kinsmen, Thomas Lee, had served as President of the Colony of Virginia, two others (Francis Lightfoot Lee and Richard Henry Lee) had already gained legendary status as the only pair of brothers who signed the Declaration of Independence. In addition, Lee's own father, Henry "Light-Horse Harry" Lee, had been a brilliant commander

Congressman Henry "Lighthorse-Harry" Lee eulogizing George Washington in Congress, Philadelphia, Pennsylvania

of cavalry during that same stuggle for liberation from the British Crown.

A close friend of George Washington, Light-Horse Harry had been awarded a Congressional Gold Medal, was three times the Governor of Virginia and a member of Congress. Of course, he was also the speaker who provided the moving eulogy at Washington's funeral, while delivering the immortal phrase that described Washington as "first in war, first in peace, and first in the hearts of his countrymen."

In the end, however, Robert Edward Lee's own career as a military man and educator would far surpass that of his legendary father, who had been a national hero.

As a child, Robert E. Lee would grow toward adolescence on the streets of Alexandria—and would be surrounded by endless reminders of that small Potomac River town's most famous citizen, George Washington. How many kids, after all, could boast that their parents had received a letter of wedding congratulations from the Father of their Country?

But he could! And for young Robert, it was a priceless family heirloom. Living in the family home on downtown Cameron Street, he soon discovered that he was at the very center of American history; these graceful old Alexandria streets had been traveled by at least half the signers of the Declaration of Independence at one time or another. (Lee, himself, was related to five of the signers through the Lees and the Carters.)

Before long the youthful Lee would be reading about the great historical struggles of the preceding generation, as a beginning student at the family's private school, "Eastern View." And it would be as an eager young student, only 11 years old, that he would be forced to endure one of the greatest losses of his life: the death of his father, in March of 1818.

Yet the courageous lad had barely had time to properly grieve, before his sister Ann's worsening health and the ever-increasing invalidism of his mother required him to shoulder an immense burden of family leadership.

For more than a year, this often worried and very serious child would receive his schooling at home—between visits for rest and recreation to his extended families at such favorite retreats as Ravensworth (where the Fitzhughs lived) and Stratford (by now the home of his half-brother, Henry). At last, however, the fast-growing Robert would enter the Alexander Academy (1820) to begin his classical studies in earnest ... and would remain there for three years, before finally sitting down to begin thinking about college.

Within a few days, a brilliant idea came to him: if his brother Smith had chosen the Navy for a career, and seemed to be happy with that choice, why couldn't Robert sign on with the Army? After all, he seemed to be quite good at math ... surely they would find a place for the son of "Light-Horse Harry" Lee at the U.S. Military Academy at West Point!

After the Lees succeeded in arranging for many of the most influential people in Virginia to recommend Robert the stage was set; he was going to be a military officer.

How eager he was to share the good news with everybody! And what a large, extended family it was ... with the vast ranks of Robert Lee's relatives and friends scattered halfway across Virginia and Maryland. As a child, Robert Lee had moved frequently between his ancestral homes in Virginia—Shirley and Stratford Hall. And later, after his marriage, he and his growing family would pay frequent visits to the other homes of his many relatives ... including such memorable and historic edifices as Ravensworth, Cedar Grove, and White House (where George and Martha Washington had been married).

But one of Lee's favorite destinations for these lively and deeply satisfying family gatherings soon became "Goodwood"—the tall, white-columned, rural brick mansion that served as headquarters for the Southern Maryland-based family of Charles Henry Carter.

As one of Maryland's leading families, the Carters were doubly related to the Lees ... both through Charles Henry's father (who was Robert Lee's uncle) *and* through Charles Henry's mother (who was Robert Lee's half-sister).

Bernard Moore Carter and his wife Lucy Grymes Lee Carter. Bernard Carter was the uncle of Robert E. Lee and Lucy Carter was Robert E. Lee's half-sister. They were the parents of Charles Henry Carter.

(Amusingly, Robert Lee's and Charles Henry's wives were *also* cousins, since they were both descendants of the Calverts, the founding family of Maryland.)

If all of this sounds impossibly complicated, it will help to understand one basic fact about life among the 19th-Century gentry of Maryland: Most of the time, these young people tended to marry others of their same class. (As a result, the same names tend to show up over and over again on local marriage registers.)

During his long and deeply affectionate relationship with the "Carters of Goodwood," Robert E. Lee would write scores of letters to his Maryland relatives ... the vast majority of them to his Cousin Charles, and to two of Charles' six daughters, Annette and Ella.

Along with revealing a great deal of Robert E. Lee's "psychology" —as a warm-hearted, kindly gentleman who loved to tease his beautiful cousins, while praising them to the skies—the letters make clear one key fact that has often been overlooked in histories of the period: like most other citizens of the mid-Atlantic region, Robert E. Lee considered Maryland a Southern state ... and he fully expected this hotbed of Confederate sympathizers to fight on the side of Jefferson Davis and Robert E. Lee.

Indeed, one of the most remarkable letters, penned by Lee on January 16, 1861, to "Cousin Annette," makes this point with crystal clarity. ("Annette, tell your father he must not allow Maryland to be tacked on to S. Carolina before the just demands of the South have been fairly presented to the North and rejected!") And several of the other "Carter Letters" suggest that just about everybody in Robert Lee's world fully expected Maryland to side with the South.

But the "Carter Letters" speak of many other subjects, as well. Again and again, they show us the informal, gentle and very human side of General Lee—a man who placed family values and love of kin above all other values in human life.

Listen to the 52-year-old Colonel, as he looks forward to his next leisurely visit to Goodwood. Written while Lee was on Federal assignment in nearby Washington City, this letter of March 12, 1859, was composed by a man who stood on the edge of a precipice, as he watched the nation he loved careening toward certain disaster.

Yet Lee's concerns on this day are entirely with his family members; in line after line, he talks about his strong desire to be with his own kin—including, especially, Cousins Charles, Ella and Annette.

Arlington 12 March, '59

I am delighted, my beautiful Annette, at the prospect of seeing you soon, & also that you will accompany us to the wedding. I have been trying all this winter to get to Goodwood, but since December have been constantly on some Military Court or board from which I could not escape.

At one time during an interval between them, I had determined to go down with the girls on a Friday & return Monday, but Mr. Hill whom I met as I came from the adjournment of the Court, said the roads were impossible for a carrige & that he was obliged to go on horseback. The next morning also we had another hard rain—that prevented Rooney and I from going on horseback.

I am still engaged on a Mil. Board, but expect to finish Monday or Tuesday. Tell Sweet Ella [Carter] & your dear Papa [Charles Henry Carter] why I have not been down. After the wedding I must prepare for [cavalry duty in] Texas.

But I hope to see you all before I go. You at any rate Annita will be up next week. You must not make it later than Saturday next (18th), as we are as yet uncertain of the days the steamer leaves Richmond for Shirley & may have to go from here Monday. Uncle Wms who is here says we must do so, but I have written to ascertain the time.

I know you will be the most beautiful dressed person at the wedding. Still you may have to get some ribbons for the occasion. Come up therefore as early as you can. If I knew the day I would meet you in W.

Fitzhugh will be home tonight.

Give much love to your father & Ella & believe me truly

Your Cousin
R.E. Lee [3]

The Revolt Begins In Maryland

When Robert E. Lee wrote that letter to his Cousin Annette in 1859, the Maryland landscape that he loved so much was facing a dire threat—not from some foreign invader, but from the Federal government of the United States. By 1860, in fact, much of the populace of the Old Line State had become convinced that the continuing Federal abuse of "States rights" could not be tolerated further—and that secession was the only realistic course of action for the violated Southern states.

And indeed, even a brief look at the Presidential vote tallies in Maryland in 1860 shows how strong this "anti-Federal" and "anti-Lincoln" sentiment was running. The totals showed that the Democratic National Party's John C. Breckinridge had won the state with a hefty 46 percent of the vote (in a four-way race), while the Republican candidate and eventual national winner, Abraham Lincoln, drew only a microscopic 2 and ½ percent. (In two Maryland counties, Worcester and Queen Anne's, Lincoln received not a single vote.)

In "Maryland–The South's First Casualty," Bart Rhett Talbert tells of the rejection of Lincoln in Maryland: "Maryland cast her vote for the Southern Democrats and, like her sister state of Virginia, showed strong support for the conservative, pro-slavery Constitutional Unionists. This display of Southern Conservatism unquestionably rejected Lincoln and his sectional party, which prevailed by a majority of electoral votes of the exclusively Northern states.

"Lincoln received 1,857,610 votes out of just less than 5 million cast, which meant that less than four out of every ten men voted Republican. Through its power in the electoral college, a minority of Republican voters in the North had elected a President that three million American voters had rejected."

At Goodwood, as elsewhere in Maryland, informed citizens at every level of society were already predicting that the Southern states would begin to secede, sometime in 1860.

Nor was there any doubt, in most quarters, that Maryland would be among them ... or that the step toward secession was a step toward a revolution that would end in blood.

And yet life went on as before. For Robert E. Lee, the endless hours of work in Washington would soon be replaced by endless cavalry marches across the flat, dust-swirling parade ground at Fort Mason, near San Antonio ... where he would be stationed until February, 1861, before returning to Arlington.

But not now. Not yet. For now, between the military court sessions in Washington, there was always Goodwood to look forward to. There was dancing in the great central ballroom of the mansion that George Calvert had built in 1799; there were picnics and croquet and leisurely strolls across the soft grass of the immense front lawn.

To read Robert E. Lee's correspondence from this era is to watch a man celebrate the beauty and joy of life—while standing at the edge of a yawning abyss. Listen to him on 14 June, 1859, in one of the many letters he would write to Cousin Annette at Goodwood.

Arlington 14 June '59

My beautiful Annette

I am so disappointed you did not come up with your father. There was a nice seat for you in the buggy, & we should have enjoyed your Company much more than the wedding party tonight. I shall not let you suppose that you have got rid of me by staying at home, for I shall not go to Texas till I see you. So you had better Come up at once & be done with it. When are you coming, for I want to see your sweet face badly?

Your father will inform you that our young party left this morning for Cedar Grove. May Childs accomp'd them. Fitzhugh & Charlotte were to have been of the party, but our Uncle Wms & their Grnfather arrived yesterday to pay them a visit, which kept them at home. It is probable they may follow in the next boat. They will all return next week. Mary C proposed going to Goodwood with Ella & I hope you will return with her. Do come. It has been so long since you were here.

We have no flowers now to show you but the grass is very green & the wood very shady. The sight of you I am sure would benefit Agnes' eyes, who longs much for your Company. She & Annie have been busy of late preparing some summer dresses, & your skill in Cutting would have been of vast assistance to them. I do not think they will ever be able to Compete with you.

Mary Carter did not come on with the other Marys. Her heart failed her when the time arrived for their departure. She could not leave the dear Dr. I understand they are not to be married till his practice, now very slim, is sufficient to ensure a support.

Lizzie Carter & Mr John Wickham are positively engaged. Her mother told Henry Turner so, who was here the other day & was just from Shirley. Mr. Wm Wickham also informed me, as I passed through Hanover. There is therefore no doubt of it. Have there been any more letters from Hilly?

Mary Lee has one of her West Point friends staying with her, Mrs. Barnes, whose husband is a surgeon in the Army & is now in California. She was a Miss Fauntleroy of Vrga. I think she looks very complacently upon your father.

I have told you all the news, but I cannot tell you how much I long to see you & how much I have to tell you. You must see that for yourself. The girls left much love for you & with mine for Mildred.

> I remain truly
> Your Cousin
> R.E. Lee

Miss Annette Carter [4]

And so the music played on at Goodwood, as it had been playing since that glorious year of 1830—when Charles Henry Carter had married the daughter of George Calvert, Rosalie Eugenia Calvert, and then had moved his new family to the 728-acre plantation estate at Queen Anne.

Located only 20 miles east of Washington on a hill overlooking the bottomland of the Patuxent River, Goodwood would serve as family headquarters for the Carters of Maryland throughout the coming storm.

Ardent supporters of the Confederacy during all the agonizing years of the war, the Carters would also remain utterly loyal to her greatest general, their Cousin Robert E. Lee.

To understand how close these two families eventually became, one needs only to read a letter written by Robert E. Lee's mother, Ann Carter Lee, concerning Charles Henry and his sisters in 1827, while Robert was attending West Point. *"Alas, alas,"* Mrs. Lee wrote, *"I wish I had my little boys Smith and Robert living with me again.*

"My brother Bernard's three elder daughters and Capt. Henry spent the last four months with us. They are accomplished pretty girls, Mildred is quite a beauty, Charles is also a handsome man, very Honorable and correct. ..." [5]

Goodwood! As the years passed, the two families continued their delightful visits. The music played on, the dancers whirled and whirled, and the distant rumble of the approaching thunder went unheard. ...

CHAPTER TWO

Lee at West Point

I am impelled to make special mention of the services of Captain R.E. Lee, engineers. This officer, greatly distinguished at the siege of Vera Cruz, was again indefatigable during these operations, in reconnaissance as daring as laborious, and of the utmost value. Nor was he less conspicuous in planting batteries, and in conducting columns to their stations under the heavy fire of the enemy.

—General Winfield Scott, Commander of the American Army in Mexico, describing Robert E. Lee's heroism at the battle of Cerro Gordo in the Mexican War of 1846–48.

West Point.

A breezy, mellow, sunshine-filled afternoon in the merry month of May. In the distance, a platoon of young soldiers marches back and forth across the main "parade deck," here at the nation's foremost academy for the education and training of U.S. Army officers.

It's springtime, 1854, and the legendary Superintendent—accompanied by his 18-year-old cousin from Goodwood, in Maryland, the delightful Miss Ella Carter—has come out to watch the troops at their afternoon drill.

"Left ... left ... one, two, three, gimme your *left!*"

Now the Platoon Commander barks furiously at his youthful charges: "Dress it up, dress it up—first rank, bring it up, I said *dress* that line up ... left, your left, one, two three. ..."

Standing on the slope of the great hill that flanks the parade deck, the Colonel can't help smiling.

Can't help remembering his *own* years at West Point—the years when he, too, had been a callow, eager young man burning with military ambition, burning with his dream of a heroic military career. Those years (1825–29) when the slender, brown-eyed young man from Alexandria, Virginia, had blazed like a meteor through his four years at "The Academy" ... while ranking at the head of his class in artillery and winning the coveted post of "Adjutant of the Corps" during his senior year.

As a lad from Virginia whose father—"Light-Horse Harry" Lee—was shrouded in the legend of his Revolutionary War exploits, young Robert had faced a mighty challenge at the U.S. Military Academy: could he establish himself as an outstanding military officer on his own merits?

Could the slender young man from Cameron Street prove to the world that he deserved the title of "Light-Horse Harry's Boy"?

He could. He did. From beginning to end, Lee's performance at West Point had been nothing short of breathtaking: a virtuoso career in which his high marks in the classroom (in mathematics, in French, in engineering and in several other subjects) had been surpassed only by his award-winning accomplishments in artillery school, and his impeccable, demerit-free record for "good conduct."

Listed as a "Distinguished Cadet" upon his graduation in 1829, and ranked second in his graduating class, Lee had been fully prepared for the extraordinary military career that was to follow—a career in which his contribution as a Captain of Engineers would be exceeded only by his heroism during several major battles in the struggle with Mexico.

Now, as he strolled back and forth with his Goodwood cousin beneath the bright blue skies of this gentle spring afternoon, Lee understood all over again why he loved this military life of his, this special destiny. Yes, gazing upon Ella's smiling face, as she tilted her bright yellow sunshade and bared her pretty features to the sky, it was quite easy for the 47-year-old Colonel to remember his *own* youth, his own joyful aspirations, so many years ago, when he himself had marched back and forth across this green-washed plain. ...

"Gimme your left, your left, one-two-three! ..."

Smiling happily in the sunshine, he watched the platoon step smartly through a left-flanking movement, then pivot back into place. The quest for perfection! What had Robert E. Lee's own life been, if not a continuing quest for this kind of excellence? And what else could anyone have expected, given the unique circumstances of his birth ... not only as the son of Light-Horse Harry, but also as a cousin of two signers of the Declaration of Independence-Richard Henry and Francis Lightfoot Lee.

Destiny.

History! Why, Thomas Jefferson, himself, had still been in the White House while young Robert was a tiny tot at fabled Stratford Hall! And then a few years later, while the child was sitting in his wooden desk in the local gradeschool in Alexandria, there had been that terrible disturbance as the British burned Washington, before going down to ignominious defeat in the War of 1812.

Of course, Robert's famous father had been caught up in his own kind of terrible war, by then ... struggling with the huge business debts that were the result of his impulsive nature. In the end, he'd lost the splendid Stratford mansion (a "lifetime right" from his first wife, Matilda Lee, who would pass it on to her own son, Henry), and had been forced to move the entire family to Alexandria.

Although he was worshipped by the Lee children, the war hero simply had no head for business; while his loyal second wife Ann Carter Lee (Robert's mother) watched in stricken horror, the old soldier endured one financial catastrophe after the next. Then, with the creditors banging almost daily at the family's door on Cameron Street, poor Light-Horse had been struck even harder by misfortune—in a pointless act of violence, he'd been beaten nearly to death by an inflamed mob in Baltimore, at the height of the War of 1812.

By the time young Robert had entered grade school, his father was only a memory: having obtained special permission from President James Madison, a Princeton classmate of Light-Horse, the valorous old warrior had headed for the British West Indies, where he hoped to rebuild his finances and regain his health. But it was not to be: Light-Horse would die of an illness in 1818, at Cumberland Island off the coast of Georgia, while struggling to return to the family he had always loved so passionately.

Buried with a 13-gun salute and lavish funeral services at the home of his old friend and Revolutionary War commander, the departed General Nathaniel Greene, Light-Horse belonged now to the ages ... and to the aching, sorrowful place that Robert E. Lee would discover in his own heart, whenever he heard that poignant word: Father.

He would never see the great cavalryman again.

And yet the grief of this early loss—one of several that the boy would be forced to endure—had been assuaged, at least a bit, by the brand-new, childhood friendships he was building with his energetic, happy-go-lucky cousins, the Carter clan!

As a thoughtful but physically active youth who was already surging toward his adult height of nearly six feet, the "Lee boy" always got a terrific charge out of playing with his Carter kin ... and especially out of his wrestling matches and foot-races with Charles Henry Carter, three years his senior. Whether playing ball with Charles Henry at "Shirley," Robert's mother's ancestral home, or racing back and forth across the playground at the Eastern View school (the Carter boys all studied there, while the girls attended school at Shirley), Robert and Charles Henry had simply become inseparable.

How pleasing, how utterly perfect, that Charles Henry's daughter Ella would be standing beside him now, smiling beneath her yellow parasol, as the troops marched back and forth across the West Point grass! What a pleasant reminder she was of the closeness and loyalty that these two branches of Robert E. Lee's family had always felt for each other!

And indeed, Robert had needed that close connection, had needed it desperately, soon after his own graduation from West Point in 1829, when his invalid-mother, worn out by the stress of a lifetime of caring for her brood almost singlehandedly, had finally succumbed.

He was 22 years old, and now parentless ... but Ann Carter Lee had always impressed one crucial fact on him: "There is nothing more important than family!" And now that teaching would save him: for in spite of his pain, he knew he still had his brothers and sisters, and he still had Charles Henry and those Maryland cousins!

Somehow, he swallowed back his grief, picked up the pieces of his life, and began to answer the call of "sublime duty"—the call that required a young officer from West Point to begin serving the American Army that had spent so much time and money and energy in training him.

He began to answer that call first at Cockspur Island in the Savannah River, where he would earn distinction as part of the elite Corps of Engineers.

And how exciting it had been, to rise each morning with the military bugles, and button on that proud uniform, and hurry through a quick stop at the mess hall ... before setting out on that day's round of engineering and construction duties.

Exciting, also, was the sudden visit in 1830 from his pal and loyal cousin, the glowing Charles Henry—who had a smiling young woman, his brand-new bride (Rosalie Eugenia Calvert Carter), in tow.

How glorious it had been for the three of them, paddling happily about on the bottle-green Savannah, to plan and dream together about the marvelous future that awaited both the Lee and the Carter clans! Indeed, so impressed had the young Lieutenant Lee been with these nuptial-blessed visitors that he'd dashed off a quick letter to his brother, Carter, almost as soon as they departed on the steamer:

"You never saw a fellow take a thing more kindly than Sweet Charles does his marriage. There is not a party of any kind afloat, but what he is figuring away [dancing] in his black tights and white silks, dancing and flirting with all the girls, while the madam is left at home to take care of her health." [6]

And indeed, the joy that Robert was witnessing would be the precursor of his own: within a year or so of that Savannah visit from the Carter newlyweds, Robert E. Lee would be marrying a young woman named Mary Randolph Custis, at Arlington, her family home in Northern Virginia.

A great-granddaughter of Martha Washington and also the daughter of George Washington Parke Custis, Lee's new wife was the product of an aristocratic family whose noble bloodlines fully matched his own.

After all, hadn't her father been born at the Calvert mansion of Mt. Airy, over in Prince George's County, Maryland ... and then brought up at Mt. Vernon, where he'd been adopted by none other than George Washington? And hadn't George Washington Custis then gone on to build mighty "Arlington"—one of the great "plantation houses" of that era—in Northern Virginia, only a few miles south of Washington?

Arlington would now become Robert E. Lee's home; it would also provide the extraordinary, glittering backdrop for one of the most celebrated weddings ever to be staged by Virginia society. Among other notables, the guest list included "the Marshalls, the Carters, the Fitzhughs, the Tayloes and other first families of Virginia."

With Rosalie Eugenia Carter's sister, Julia Calvert, serving as a bridesmaid, the joyful festivities lasted for several days (a common custom at the time, among these Southern aristocrats), and everyone said the same thing: wasn't it wonderful to see how the handsome young Army engineer had forever joined, by marriage, the family of America's founding father, George Washington?

The joyful tidings of that happy day would be muted, though, about two months later—with the sudden explosion in Virginia of

Charles Henry Carter

what became known as the "Nat Turner incident." Who could explain what had gotten into this crazed renegade ... or into the band of 70 slaves who'd briefly joined him in the bloody insurrection, "Nat Turner's Rebellion," in which 57 men, women and children had been mercilessly slaughtered?

From beginning to end, it had been a ghastly affair. Captured within six weeks, Turner and his fellow-conspirators had been hanged at Jerusalem, Virginia. But there was no mistaking the meaning of this chilling event—or the shudder of terror that went through slaveholders everywhere in the days that followed it. Within a matter of hours, it seemed, Southern legislators everywhere were introducing new laws aimed at keeping on the lid on the boiling pot that was slavery.

But these draconian measures would find no friend in Robert E. Lee, whose anti-slavery convictions had been made clear again and again throughout his life. As he wrote to Mrs. Lee, in one particularly eloquent commentary on the subject: *"In this enlightened age there are few, I believe, but will acknowledge that slavery as an institution is a moral and political evil in any country."*

And indeed, Lee remained convinced throughout his life that Providence would eventually free the slaves of the South, and that their own well-being required that they be assimilated into the surrounding white society slowly and patiently.

Like his friends and family, Lee had hoped against hope that the Nat Turner tragedy would never be repeated. And yet it became quite clear during the early 1830's that the growing tension between the Southern way of life (agrarian, and based on slavery) and the Northern mode of living (based on industry and trade) would someday explode into open conflict.

Who could conclude otherwise, in 1832, when the patriots of South Carolina introduced legislation designed to end tariffs that "protected" Northern manufacturing—at the expense of the agrarian South?

That early crisis, of course, had brought great notoriety to "States-Righter" John Calhoun, who fought furiously to wipe out the preferential tariffs. And the growing crisis had been averted only at the last moment, when Henry Clay's Compromise Tariff of 1833 de-fused a looming military confrontation, and kept the danger of an outright military collision at bay for a few more years.

Still, the damage had been done. By now, any thoughtful observer of the youthful Republic understood the obvious: something had to give, if armed conflict between North and South were to be avoided in the future. And the reasons for that budding conflict lay, as always, in the troubled history of the two regions—lay, first of all, in the simple fact that between 1791 and 1837, 13 states had joined the Union—seven of them southern, and six northern. (By 1837, there would be 13 states representing each region.)

During the early years, of course, the struggling Congress had managed to keep a balance between the "slave" and "non-slave" states ... an important accomplishment, since it prevented one region from dominating the other, and thus triggering open hostilities.

But by the late 1840's and early 1850's, it was becoming quite evident to the Southern leaders that the North was attempting to overturn this pattern of compromise and balance ... mainly by prohibiting slavery in the new American "territories," as each one applied for statehood.

Regardless of the intricacies of the debate, the Southern loyalists understood one fact with crystal clarity: if the "territories" came into the Union in the non-slavery mode, the balance of power in the country would quickly shift in favor of the industrialists of the North.

And sooner or later, the North would then use its majority in the Senate to pass the hated "tariff laws" that would assure the North of national domination for decades to come.

This, then, was the backdrop against which a youthful Army engineering officer named Robert E. Lee spent the early years of his marvelously successful career—years in which he would serve at a dozen different outposts (mainly in the midwest), while slowly transforming himself into one of the most effective commanders in the Army Corps of Engineers.

Meanwhile, starting around 1830, Robert's beloved Maryland cousin, Charles Henry Carter, would be establishing himself as a leader in his own world: the world of the great "Southern plantation farmers" of the mid-Atlantic region.

Having married Rosalie Eugenia Calvert in 1830 in Philadelphia, Charles had carried her home to "Goodwood"—the Maryland mansion at Queen Anne (located only a few miles from Upper Marlborough)—which had been a gift from Rosalie Eugenia's father, George Calvert, famous throughout the region as the proprietor of "Riversdale."

In 1836, in fact, the kindly Calvert would deed the plantation outright to his daughter and son-in-law. And what a gift it was: 728 acres of rich, black bottomland, along with the two-story, Federal-style "Goodwood" manor house, with its 42 slaves, that was to become such a major landmark in the life and times of Robert E. Lee.

How many times, in the long years that lay ahead, would Robert and the "Maryland Cousins" enjoy together the natural splendors of this shady, tree-lined estate, as they walked the intricate gardens and ambled along on horseback down the winding bridal paths of what was undoubtedly one of Maryland's most sumptuous mansions!

Interestingly enough, Robert E. Lee would actually sign the deed-of-transfer that brought Goodwood to his cousin ... and would thus end up as one of the "trustees" for the property.

While the country around him continued to bicker and quarrel over its national destiny, young Officer Lee of the U.S. Army Corps of Engineers was doing his best to focus squarely on the task at hand. And as always, the results were solidly impressive: By 1837, the hard-charging engineer would be helping to direct the crucially important navigational improvements that were being made to the Mississippi River.

In 1840, with Lee having been promoted to Captain and the Mississippi project well in hand, he would take a leave of absence and return to Arlington ... where he would agree, among other tasks, to serve as executor of his Uncle Bernard's will, along with Bernard's own son, Charles Henry.

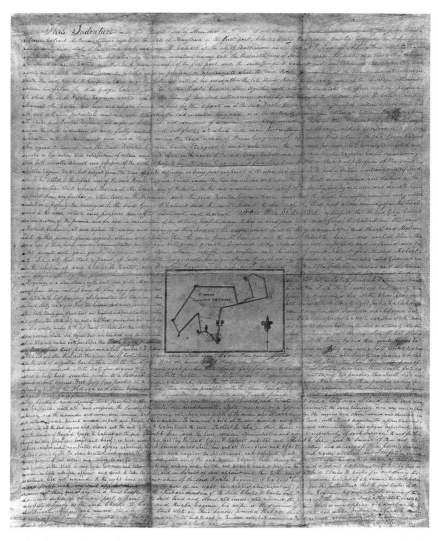

Deed of Goodwood, Queen Anne, Prince George's County, Maryland.
(Courtesy Maryland Historical Society)

Goodwood deed

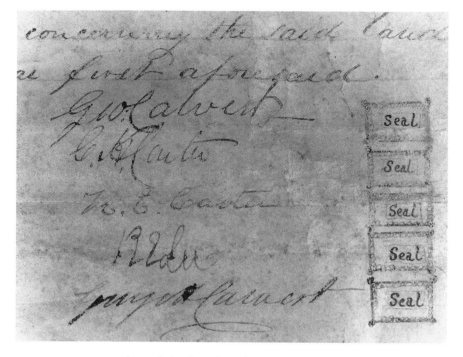

Goodwood deed with Robert E. Lee signature

Bernard M. Carter, Esq.
Philadelphia, Penn.

Washington, 10 June 1840

My dear Uncle

I have just read your letter of yesterday's date informing me that you had appointed Charles & myself your sole Executors & have deposited your "will" with Miss: Thos. Biddle & Co. of Philadelphia subject to be delivered to either of us on our personal application or order.

I shall endeavor my dear uncle so far as lies in my power to carry out fully your wishes & directions in all things, & at the same time trust that it will be long, very long before I shall be called on to exercise these duties.

I hope your determination to sail for Europe had not been caused by unfavourable intelligence of your affairs abroad, but rather by your convenience or pleasure.

Old York [probably a favorite family slave] is in fine health & spirits & looks better than when you left here. I have written to Bernard for directions concerning him but have not yet heard from or of him, neither have I heard from Carter since your departure.

We are all well at Arlington. The Servis left us yesterday—Mrs. F. is well at Ravensworth.

Very truly & Affectionately,
R.E. Lee [7]

For Captain Lee and his engineers, the late 1830's were indeed a busy time. Soon after his visit to Arlington, the engineering wizard was posted on to Forts Lafayette and Hamilton, in New York. After arriving there in April of 1841 and being joined by his own family, Lee learned some tragic news: his Uncle Bernard had passed away. Lee would respond instantly, with a moving letter to Charles at Goodwood:

Charles H. Carter, Esq.
Queen Anne, P. George's, Md.

> *Ft. Hamilton, N.Y.*
> *7 March 1842*
> *Monday night*

My dear Charles

I have this moment received your letter of the 4th inst. conveying the sad intelligence of your dear father's death. Had it reached me in time, I should certainly have been with you to have assisted in the melancholy offices of his funeral from which I have been detained by our receiving here no mail on Sunday.

We have indeed all lost a friend and you the best of fathers. But his troubles and sorrows have now ceased and his happiness I trust will now be forever. Our loss has been his gain and we must not be selfish enough to ———[illegible]

It would be impossible for me to reach Phil. before your departure. Matilda in her letter seemed to think that my presence would be necessary, but I cannot think so, as I understand that it was only in case of your absence or death that I would be called onto to act, and your silence on the subject confirms me in my opinion.

> *Very truly c- **R.E. Lee*** [8]

Returning to Washington by April of 1842, Lee spent some time comforting his Cousin Charles at Arlington—before giving him a letter that terminated his (Lee's) "co-executorship" of Bernard's will. In that letter, Captain Lee reminds Charles of his "filial" devotion to Uncle Bernard ... of whom Robert, like his mother, had been very fond (his "Uncle B").

Arlington 13 April 1842

My dear Charles

I enclose my letter of resignation as joint Executor & trustee, in which I have desired to embody my reasons for declining lest I might be thought to have been governed by a wish to save myself trouble.

From the almost filial affection with which I have always regarded your dear father, I would have most cheerfully have undertaken the trust did I not conscientiously believe that the interests of his children required my declining.

The whole matter now devolves on you, the best qualified as well as well as the most proper person to undertake it. I trust that your success in the management of the property may be equal to your wishes and anxiety concerning it.

> *Very truly & affectionately yours,*
> *R.E. Lee* [9]

While reading these letters to Charles Henry Carter about the death of his father, it's easy to imagine the swirling current of feelings that must have been raging through Robert E. Lee—on that mellow May afternoon in 1854 when he stood above the plain at West Point with Charles' 18-year-old daughter, Ella, and watched the young men go zipping through their paces: "Your left ... your right ... dress it up ... gimme your *left!*"

While the troops marched back and forth on the greensward and Ella strolled about under her parasol, Colonel Lee must also have been remembering that awful day in January of 1845, when he first learned of the terrible blow that had struck the Carters, with the death of Ella's mother, Rosalie Eugenia.

Suddenly, the world had seemed a lot colder, after the merciless subtraction of this "loving spirit" from Lee's and the Carters' lives. As Eugenia's mother, Rosalie Eugenia Stier Calvert, had written when Ella's mother was herself only a child: "*She is so good, so lovable, so happy that she is everyone's favorite. It is impossible to see her without loving her. ... If I had the power of fairies, I could add nothing to her person or her character."*

A direct descendant of Lord Baltimore, and a granddaughter of the esteemed Stier family, Eugenia was also descended from the great Dutch painter Peter Paul Rubens. But now she was gone forever, at age 39, and would be buried in the rich soil of Goodwood ... after leaving behind six daughters and a son, along with the grieving Charles Henry.

Robert's cousin would never remarry; along with the sorrowful children, the loyal Charles would spend more and more time at Cedar Grove, the home of his sister-in-law, Julia Stuart, in Virginia. Aunt Julia Calvert Stuart would do her best to comfort all of them, of course ... but the children (who ranged in ages from two-year-old Mary through 13-year-old Eugenia) would be affected forever, even though Julia did her best to become a "surrogate mother" for all of them.

Destiny.

While registering the first shock of that terrible loss, Lee would write to his inconsolable cousin from Arlington.

Arlington 17 Jany 1845

My dear Charles

The papers of last night gave us the first information of the terrible misfortune that has befallen you, nor had we before any intimation that it was impending. Our grief for your distress was not lessened by the shock of our own feelings. We deeply sympathize with you and fully appreciate your incomparable loss.

None could have a higher esteem or sincere affection for your dear wife than ourselves. As her loss is so painful to us we know how agonizing it is to you.

I wish I could give you any consolation. She however is free from care & pain & at peace in heaven. God grant that we may all meet her there &

that you & your sweet children may mutually comfort each other in your great distress.

I arrived here before New Years, where I was ordered on duty. We are all well & all join me in much love to yourself & children. Can't you bring them up to see us?

R.E. Lee

Chas. H. Carter Esq. [10]

The Battle For Mexico: A Legend Is Born

Walking back and forth along the "observation deck" with the lovely Ella Carter, Colonel Lee must have found himself blinking back the tears, as he recalled the tragic loss of her mother, Rosalie Eugenia. And his emotion would have been perfectly understandable: having been deprived of his own parents far too early in life, the southern gentleman in the elegant gray coat understood all too well the agonizing grief that had overwhelmed the youthful Ella, soon after her mother's death.

And yet life goes on.

Somehow, with the aid of Providence, ordinary life resumes.

Ella had survived; now, walking with her cousin above the parade ground at West Point, she was the very image of youthful pulchritude: a charming young woman smiling beneath a bright parasol, while the daring, slim-waisted soldiers marched smartly before her.

Life goes on!

In Lee's case, also, the resumption of ordinary affairs—the return to public "duty"—must have come as a distinct relief, after the misery of watching Cousin Charles confront his bleak future without a beloved wife.

Heartbreak. After witnessing so much tragic loss and sorrow within the circle of his own family, the Captain of Engineers must have been almost pleased to discover that the forces of history were about to call him away from hearth and home, and to provide him with a distraction that would soon plunge him headlong into the middle of the great military showdown that dominated the middle years of the 19th Century: the Mexican War.

Like every military conflict, the War with Mexico had its roots buried deep in the past. Was it already a decade since those brave Texans had revolted against the Mexican government of the dictator General Antonio Lopez de Santa Anna, while declaring that they wanted nothing so much as to become self-governing, in all the regions north of the sluggish Rio Grande?

Was it already a decade, by 1846, since the same despised Santa Anna had stormed that tiny, virtually defenseless fort at San Antonio—The Alamo—and wiped out the heroic garrison there, in a battle that ended only with the death of the last standing American?

Yes: By the summer of 1846, when Captain Lee was ordered to join the Americans fighting south of the border, Texas had already been enjoying statehood for more than a year.

But the endless border disputes in the region—most of them centering on the contested territory adjacent to the Rio Grande—had been flaring again and again into brutal fire-fights, most of which consisted of American troops being attacked by Mexican ambushers in the scrubby hill-country that flanked the watercourse.

Enraged finally to the point of action, the Americans had formally declared war against Santa Anna and his thugs in May of 1846; Captain Lee's summons to battle had not been issued until late that August.

Eager for his first taste of actual warfare, the anxious Captain had finally caught up with his commander—Brigadier General John E. Wool—in late September, at San Antonio de Bexar ... only to discover that his first assignment would require picks and shovels more than musket and cannon: Lee was to direct road-building during General Wool's invasion of Mexico.

And what followed was hardly a glamorous saga: during the next few weeks and months, Captain Lee would spend endless hours repairing bridges and smoothing roads, as the thousands of infantrymen in Wool's expeditionary force marched through the dust of north and central Mexico.

It would be March of 1847, in fact, before Lee would hear a shot fired in anger. By then, of course, he would have joined the great General Winfield Scott outside Vera Cruz, as part of the invasion force that would capture that graceful old city. For the first time in his forty years, the Virginia gentleman was facing down actual gunfire; in one celebrated incident, a whistling round passed so close that it actually singed his jacket.

After two days of artillery duels—the American batteries were organized and maintained by Engineer Lee—the Mexicans sent up a white flag, and Vera Cruz capitulated.

Suddenly, Lee was receiving lavish praise in the military dispatches of General Scott and the other commanders, as a key figure in the attack who had performed "noble service."

But the action was only beginning.

On the morning of April 15, 1847, at a mountain pass near the Rio del Plan, Lee would endure a hair-raising experience that no soldier could ever hope to forget.

Scott wanted a reconnaissance of the narrow, scrubby ravines that flanked the river ... a bleak bottleneck where, according to several intelligence reports, Santa Anna himself was lurking with more than 10,000 men.

As usual, Captain Lee instantly volunteered to perform that reconnaissance.

An hour later, accompanied by a guide, the Virginia soldier was inching his away along a section of steep, narrow ravines. Could he find a way to build a decent road through here—a road strong and smooth enough to allow thousands of marching soldiers an easy passage?

Sometime before noon, the advance scout reached a small spring flanked by an immense, fallen log. While his guide wandered off out of earshot, in search of signs of enemy troop movements, Lee took a drink from the spring ... then sat down on the log to make some road-building plans.

A moment later, he froze.

Clearly audible in the jungle cover, only twenty yards distant: "Que es esto?"

"No comprende! Habemos una problema?"

Several of Santa Anna's troopers were making directly for the spring!

In a flash, Lee had sprung to his feet. Wildly, he glanced around him: No escape.

There was no other choice ... with his heart hammering furiously in his chest, the engineer dropped down behind the great log, which was screened from the clearing by some heavy foliage.

The Mexicans approached the spring.

"Ah ... agua frio! Muy bueno!"

"Me gusta ... caramba ... frio!"

Stretched out full-length beside the log, the Captain held his breath. One false move, and his Mexican adventure would come to an end—permanently.

It took an eternity—maybe three or four minutes—for the troopers to drink their fill, and then move on.

Gasping with relief, the nerve-wracked Lee came up to one knee, and prepared to bolt away from the spring ... only to hear: "Aqui! El agua!"

Unbelievably, a *second* party of soldiers had now reached the bubbling fountain on the jungle floor.

Raging with inward frustration, the tormented Captain somehow managed to muffle his breathing. Slowly, he sank back into the thick, matted grasses beside the log.

But this time, the drinkers were in no great hurry to return to their unit; they stretched their "R&R" session at the spring out for a full half hour. And then, before they'd even departed the clearing, yet another band of Santa Anna's bold warriors arrived for refreshment!

And it went on like that, minute after minute and hour after hour, until twilight finally came drifting down over the tree-cover, and the exasperated Lee could finally skulk off into the underbrush, as frustrated and furious as he'd ever been in his life.

For Robert E. Lee, the Battle of Cerro Gordo began with this inauspicious debut beside a felled log. But what followed, during the next several days, was hardly the stuff of comedy: as a commander of artillery assigned to Colonel Bennett Riley's Second Brigade, he would spend those days working furiously to keep the big guns on target and firing—even as the swarming Mexicans blasted his position repeatedly from their formidable redoubt on the slopes of Cerro Gordo.

In the end Santa Anna's fortress crumbled, his defensive lines collapsed, and thousands of his troopers were either captured or cut to pieces along the blood-soaked Jalapa Road.

Describing the ghastly carnage later, a chastened Lee would write to his son Custis: "You have no idea what a horrible sight a field of battle is."

For his part, meanwhile, General Winfield Scott was already writing to Washington—about the heroic exploits of one Capt. Robert E. Lee of Engineers:

"This officer, greatly distinguished at the siege of Vera Cruz, was again indefatigable during these operations, in reconnaissance as daring as laborious, and of the utmost value."

Within a few days, Lee would be brevetted to major, and the commendation would read: "For gallant and meritorious conduct in the battle of Cerro Gordo."

For the future Confederate general, that historic battle—along with the later, more famous battle for Chapultepec, on the very outskirts of Mexico City—would provide a few, invaluable military lessons … lessons that Lee would rely on in conducting his operations during the War for Southern Independence some fifteen years later.

From General Scott, Lee would learn, for example, the crucial concept of delegating battle-fighting responsibilities to his lieutenants —while saving his own energies and skills for the more important function of planning the entire operation.

From what happened at Cerro Gordo and Chapultepec, also, Lee would conclude that nothing mattered as much in warfare as a careful reconnaissance of the terrain, before any engagement could be launched. ...

He was a veteran of combat now, this 40-year-old gentleman from Virginia: his immense education at West Point had been fully completed. And when the Mexicans finally surrendered most of Texas (north of the Rio Grande) to the Americans in February of 1848, with the Treaty of Guadalupe Hidalgo, Robert E. Lee was as skillful and accomplished a military officer as one could hope to find in the U.S. Army.

Did he suspect, even then, that when his great moment came, it would come in battles *against* that same army ... battles in which one of his staunchest fellow-soldiers at Cerro Gordo, a young infantry lieutenant named George B. McClellan, would suddenly reappear as one of Lee's greatest adversaries?

After the smoke and fury of Cerro Gordo and Chapultepec, Lee's next assignment must have seemed very tame, indeed: in November of 1848, the newly promoted Colonel reported to Baltimore to begin his latest task, as the commander of an engineering team charged with constructing several federal installations, including Fort Carroll.

As always, Colonel Lee performed his duty.

Within a few years, however, the U.S. Army decided that it had even bigger plans for the hero of the Mexican War—and tapped the tall Virginian to be the ninth Superintendent at his own alma mater, the U.S. Military Academy at West Point.

Interestingly enough, the Brevet-Colonel was not pleased by the surprise appointment: he feared that his own background and training might prove inadequate to the task of running a large, complex operation such as the one at West Point, and said as much to his military superiors in a letter written in late May of 1852:

"I learn with much regret the determination of the Secretary of War to assign me to that duty, and I fear I cannot realize his expectations in the management of an Institution requiring more skill and more experience than I command.

"Although fully appreciating the honor of the station, and extremely reluctant to oppose my wishes to the orders of the Department, yet if I be allowed any option in the matter, I would respectfully ask that some other successor than myself be appointed to the present able Superintendent."

The Army High Command listened to this argument, and immediately decided to ignore it: Lee was too accomplished as both a manager of resources and a leader of men to be prevented by his own modesty from assuming this important post.

On September 1 of 1852, the new Superintendent strode across the parade deck at West Point and accepted his commission. During the next four years, he would be credited with numerous improvements to the august old military academy … and would take enormous pride in the fact that his own cherished son, Custis Lee, was himself compiling an excellent record there, even as his father earned plaudits in the Superintendent's office.

While operating under the firm leadership of the newly installed Secretary of War, Jefferson Davis, Lee would strengthen discipline at West Point considerably—even as he worked furiously to upgrade its academic standards. And indeed, a chatty letter Lee wrote to his son Fitzhugh during this period (February 2, 1853) clearly shows how much the Superintendent was enjoying his new assignment, since it gave him the opportunity to spend time with his own family in peaceful surroundings:

"Your sister is quite well, is learning to skate. Ella Carter is going to Miss Bottoms this present half year. Custis dined with us last Saturday. …"

Family!

Is it any wonder, then, that Robert E. Lee and the youthful Ella Carter so much enjoyed their stroll along the observation deck, on

that mild May afternoon in 1854 when the troops went marching and
drilling past in their smart, crisp formations?

"Your left ... your left ... by the left flank—march!"

For the Colonel and his cousin and all the rest of the Carters and
the Lees, it was to be a brief, final interlude before the hurricane of
sectional strife began in earnest.

Lee seems to acknowledge as much, in a whimsical letter he wrote
to Ella soon after she had left West Point, following a week's visit
with her cousin/uncle Robert and his family.

West Point 10 May 1854

My beautiful Ella,

*I suppose the enclosed is from Cousin George, saying he could not find
you in the arrival of the Cars. Does he even know your name? I hope you
found Madame Sigorgius though I do not think it safe in your Cousin M.
to have entrusted you to that gay widow.*

*Come back to me you precious child you will not find anyone to love
you half as much. Custis & I had a Sad Saturday. Many of the Cadets
called to sympathize with us, but found us such poor company they soon
left us.*

*Mr. Chitz having satisfied himself that you had actually gone, & that
he would not encounter you in the weigh station himself must ————,
before any mail could have arrived with a ———— letter.*

*See what little faith you can place in the professions of these young
men. The travellers have arrived safely in Baltimore. Mary thinks her trot
is none the worse for the journey. They said they were very sorry at parting from you, but none can regret it as much as*

your Cousin R.E. Lee [11]

Letter from Robert E. Lee to Ella Carter, 1854. Pictures starting from
top left: Richard Lee, the first Lee in America; Richard Lee II, his son;
Thomas Lee, the builder of Stratford Hall and father of the Lees who
signed the Declaration of Independence; "Lighthorse-Harry" Lee, father
of Robert E. Lee, and Robert E. Lee.

CHAPTER THREE

· The Storm Approaches ·

*To the charge of the North that succession was rebellion and trea-
son, the South replied that the epithets of rebel and traitor did not
deter her from the assertion of her independence, since these same
epithets had been familiar to the ears of Washington and Hancock
and Adams and Light-Horse Harry Lee.*

—John Brown Gordan

His time at West Point had ended; for Robert E. Lee, a new and
more hectic phase of life had begun. And by April of 1855, the new
lieutenant colonel from Arlington would be fully embarked on his
next adventure—as the second-in-command of the Army's spiffy
new 2nd Cavalry, charged with "keeping the peace" along the Texas
and California frontiers.

Tapped by the Secretary of War—Jefferson Davis—for this vi-
tally important post, Lee would serve under Colonel Albert Sidney
Johnston (later killed at Shiloh), and would be ably assisted by an
obscure lieutenant named John B. Hood. But first he was to get a

long look at one of the most unhappy aspects of military life ... while spending most of the following year in a series of endless and tedious court-martial trials.

Lee took a deep breath—and did his duty.

While the soldier went about his chores, however mundane they proved to be, his young family was living life to the fullest. And indeed, even a brief look at some of the "family correspondence" that was penned during this era shows what a happy and healthy family they all were, as Lee's offspring charged through the routines of school and play with boundless energy.

One particularly interesting memoir from that era ("Growing Up In The 1850's: The Journal Of Agnes Lee," edited by Mary Custis Lee deButts) opens a fascinating window on life among the Virginia Lees. In that volume, Agnes (Lee's third daughter) wrote at the age of 14 (1855): *"We have been & returned from C.G. [Cedar Grove], which is more than sixty miles down the river. We started with Mr. Webster in the 'Columbia,' which literally pokes, found on board Cousin Eugenia Hall [Rosalie Eugenia Carter Hall] and Alice Bowie [Alice Carter Bowie] with their children & Ella Carter, who were going with us. ...*

"Cousin Eugenia has two beautiful boys; Alice's are not so pretty nor so bad, but she is lovely, the prettiest of the family."

A few weeks later, in July, Agnes would pen another note at Arlington, while describing 19-year-old Ella: *"Ella Carter has looked lovely the whole of her stay—almost as pretty as Alice did at Cedar Grove."*

Agnes' diary would continue into September, when she joined her sister, Annie, and her cousin, Annette Carter, in a marvelous new adventure: the three girls, escorted by Agnes' cousin, Charles Carter, headed off to the Staunton Academy to begin another challenging year of study.

Agnes spent that year at Staunton rooming with Cousin Annette, and they became best friends. By March of '56, Agnes would still be scribbling away about her delightful visits with family: *"Rooney spent his vacation at home, had a charming time. He & Mary were a good deal in Washington with Ella [Carter] & Margaret [Stuart]."* Later still, while zestfully describing her life at Staunton: *"Six of us are now in a room. We five are grave & reverend seniors! ... Annette & I went to a little party at Miss Eddie Bell's, had a funny time."*

Robert E. Lee would have smiled, surely, while reading such cheery observations from his upbeat daughter. And he'd have been quite pleased, also, to discover how seriously Agnes and the others took their Christian religion ... as revealed in a letter by Agnes from August of 1857, in which she tells how she and some of her cousins were "confirmed" in the Episcopal Church:

"O after many harassing doubts and wicked want of faith I dared to be confirmed & to take the communion afterwards. Annie, Mary, Ada [Stuart] & Annette took the same step." In January of 1858, she would add in a similar vein: *"It all seems a conversion amid all this pleasure, that seldom Easter time when we five cousins came forward with others to take their vows of love & duty to God."* [12]

Mrs. Lee—deeply religious—was gratified by such fervent observations. Religion played a key role in the lives of Southerners during the 19th Century ... and especially the Episcopalian religion—a fact which moved one wag of that period to note: "There are many ways to get to heaven, but a gentleman will choose the Episcopalian way."

While his large, sprawling family continued to thrive and prosper, the colonel of cavalry was galloping across the flatlands of Texas with his unit. He would turn 50 at Fort Brown ... and like the rest of the nation, would find himself increasingly preoccupied with the "slavery question."

Because Robert E. Lee never feared speaking up and saying what was on his mind, he decided that the time had come to address this supremely painful issue head-on. In a letter addressed to the newspaper in Alexandria, his family's headquarters, the Colonel laid out a terse summary of his position on the issue. Slavery was an "evil," he said, while recommending that the evil be corrected slowly, patiently:

"In this enlightened age, there are few I believe, but what will ac-knowledge that slavery as an institution is a moral & political evil in any Country. It is useless to expatiate on its disadvantages. I think it however a greater evil to the white man than to the black race, & while my feelings are strongly enlisted in behalf of the latter, my sympathies are more strong for the former.

"The blacks are immeasurably better off here than in Africa, morally, socially & physically. The painful discipline they are undergoing, is nec-essary for their instruction as a race, & I hope will prepare & lead them to better things. How long their subjugation may be necessary is known & ordered by a wise Merciful Providence.

"Their emancipation will sooner result from the mild & melting in-fluence of Christianity, than the storms & tempests of fiery Controversy. This influence though slow, is sure. The doctrines & miracles of our Saviour have required nearly two thousand years to convert but a small part of the human race, & even among the Christian nations, what gross errors still exist!

"While we see the Course of the final abolition of human Slavery is onward, & we give it the aid of our prayers & all justifiable means in our power, we must leave the progress as well as the result in his hands who sees the end; who Chooses to work by slow influences; & with whom two thousand years are but as a Single day.

"Although the Abolitionist must know this, & must See that he has neither the right or power of operating except by moral means & sua-sion, & if he means well to the slave, he must not Create angry feel-ings in the Master; that although he may not approve the mode by which it pleases Providence to accomplish its purposes, the result will nevertheless be the same; that the reasons he gives for interference in what he has no Concern, holds good for every kind of interference with our neighbors when we disapprove of their Conduct. ..."

For Lee, of course, this decision to leave the "slavery question" squarely in hands of "Providence" was right in character. Again and again in his 50 years, the colonel of cavalry had demonstrated his faith in a Divine Presence who would eventually sort out human affairs, however painful, even if the outcome lay beyond the powers of mortal understanding.

Repeatedly in Robert E. Lee's life, we see him turning to this idea of the "Providential" for consolation—especially when death intruded to take away someone whom he deeply loved. And that was precisely his response, in October of 1857, to the news that his father-in-law, George Washington Parke Custis, had succumbed to a fatal illness.

Lee grieved ... and then went on about the business of living, as we can clearly see from a letter he wrote (December 5, 1857) to his wife's cousin, Markie Williams, from the Arlington mansion where he'd returned for Custis' funeral. Describing Markie's brother, Orten Williams, the Colonel noted: *"He however is enjoying the presence of pretty Annette Carter, who has been here about a week & expects on Monday her sister Ella from Cedar Grove."*

(Later, the same Orten Williams would become an ardent suitor of Annette's friend Agnes Lee—who would turn him down, leaving Williams to become a gung-ho lieutenant in the Confederate Army, and a Southern patriot whose hanging as a "spy" by the Federals in 1863 would loom as one of the most controversial events to take place during the war, with Williams insisting to the end that he was completely innocent of the "spying" charge.)

By March of 1859, having completed both a lengthy period of service on the Texas frontier and his duties on a temporary "government board" in Washington, Lee would find himself traveling to Washington for the marriage of his son Rooney—an event described in some detail in Douglas Southall Freeman's classic biography of Lee:

"In March he traveled to Richmond and then to Shirley, the beloved old home of his mother, where on the 23rd Rooney was married to his distant cousin, Charlotte Wirkham. The wedding was the generous, old-fashioned sort, where the guests lingered long. ... The next month, Lee made a brief trip to Goodwood, his first vacation since his return to Virginia."

Was there any joy like a father's joy at the wedding of a well-loved son? Writing to his Cousin Annette Carter, now a mature young lady of 19, Lee sounded the whimsical note of a man who understands how "in springtime, a young man's fancy turns to Love" ... and who is bursting with affection for his entire family, both close and extended.

That same affection would also be in evidence, of course, when Lee wrote to the now-married Rooney at the end of May, from Arlington, and brought him up to date on several other important family matters:

... Your sister is still in Baltimore. We have been expecting her with Ella Carter, Margaret Stuart, Mary Carter & Mary Childe for some weeks. Yesterday I received a letter from Childe saying that Mary Lee, Mary Carter & Mary Childe would be here on Thursday next on the 4 1/4 P.M. train, & as no mention was made of the others I presume they have gone or are going to Cedar Grove.

I was particularly desirous of seeing Ella & shall now be disappointed. ... I proposed to Annie, the only one who could leave home, that we should ride down to Goodwood, which we reached about dark & found Charles, Mildred & Annette. They sent the next morning early for Eugenia & Alice, who came over for the day with some of their children.

I had a very pleasant time as it was the first holiday I had taken since my return from Texas. Everything was looking very beautiful. The house had been painted & done up. The trees had grown very much, & the flowers were very beautiful & pretty. [13]

One month later, Colonel Lee would write yet another letter that displays his strong affection for the members of his "Maryland family." In that missive from Arlington, dated June 28, 1859, Lee wonders if Annette will be going to Cedar Grove (the Virginia home of her Aunt Julia Calvert Stuart, a cousin of Mary Lee).

Lee goes on to suggest that Annette might come over to Arlington from Goodwood—perhaps he can drive her to Cedar Grove and

The Planters' Advocate.

By THOMAS J. TURNER.   "TRUTH ALONE IS KNOWLEDGE—KNOWLEDGE IS POWER."   TWO DOLLARS PER ANNUM

Vol. 5.   UPPER MARLBOROUGH, MARYLAND, WEDNESDAY MORNING, JUNE 15, 1859.   No. 46.

A Beautiful Story.

WHY DID THE GOVERNESS FAINT?

Selected Poetry.

THE HOME.

June 15, 1859
POLITICS OF THE DAY

We are anxious to see re-united a people divided and distracted by ten years of fierce controversy; aggression, highhanded wrong, attempted on one side; resisted and denounced with a heat and zeal that a sense of injury begets, on the other. The South has heretofore triumphantly defeated every attempt to defranchise her. Although it may have been successful for a number of years, and her success has been owing to the justice of her demands, the practicability of her measures and the unity of her people. Her present position requires no further action at this time. The whole people of this country have adopted the proposition that there shall hereafter be no interference by Congress in the domestic government of the territories.....On this declaration and this proposition the Democratic party of Maryland, as a part of the Democracy of the South, intend to stand.

The Planters Advocate

Upper Marlborough, Maryland

(Courtesy The Enoch Pratt Free Library)

ferry his wife ("Cousin M") back home? (Letters of this kind can occasionally be confusing, because Lee sometimes refers to himself as Annette's "cousin" and sometimes as her "uncle," and of course, he was both.)

At times Lee also refers to his wife as "Cousin M" or "Cousin Mary," since she was also a cousin of the girls through the Calverts.

Arlington 28 June 1859

I was too much disappointed my beautiful Annette not to see you to-day. I had hoped certainly to have done so, & looked for you anxiously all day yesterday.

When are you Coming up & when shall I see you? Are you not going down to Cedar Grove? Miss Mary expected you, and on reaching Alexa. this morning, finding you were not with the party from here, returned to Washington with Cousin Turb. to accompany him to Chantilly this hot day. Miss Mary Jones was to be of the party. Your Cousin Mary Lee, Fitzhugh & Charlotte went down this morng.

They expected you to have gone with them. Charlotte has been wishing to see you and & all expecting you.

Come over this last of the week and I will take you down next Tuesday & bring your Cousin M. back. She thought of returning the last of next week or the first of the following. Do let me see you somewhere & tell me when—I long to see you & my time is passing away so quickly.

Very truly your Cousin
R.E. Lee

P.S. Miss Mary S. left her brothers Catesby, & Lucien to go with Turb.

Miss Annette Carter [14]

Treason At Harper's Ferry

The Union is a Union of States founded upon Compact. How is it to be supposed that when different parties enter upon a compact for certain purposes, either one can disregard one provision of it and expect others to observe the rest? If the Northern States willfully and deliberately refuse to carry out their part of the Constitution, the South would be no longer bound to keep the compact. A bargain broken on one side is broken on all sides.

—Daniel Webster, 1851

It was the beginning of a great tempest.

For Robert E. Lee, the tranquil and ordered world that he had always known—the world of the "Old South"—probably began to change forever on October 17, 1859, when he encountered a man with the perfectly ordinary name of "John Brown," at an obscure federal armory located on the Potomac River at Harper's Ferry, Virginia.

The incident began harmlessly enough ... with a visit to Arlington from one of Lee's favorite lieutenants, Jeb Stuart, who carried a mysterious-looking envelope from the War Department. Tearing the missive open, the Colonel was startled to find an order requiring him to report to Washington immediately.

Apparently, there had been some sort of "civil insurrection" at Harper's Ferry, where train service had been interrupted and mobs of outsiders were reportedly preparing for a riot.

Lee was ordered to assume command of a variety of different forces, including a Marine detachment, some militia from Maryland and some regular Federal troops from nearby Fort Monroe.

After a brief consultation at the White House, Lee and Stuart hurried to Sandy Hook, about a mile from Harpers Ferry. Once there, he learned to his dismay that the insurgents—led by the fiery Brown—had taken hostages and were hunkered down within the armory grounds.

Around 11 p.m. that evening, Lee crossed the Potomac into Virginia and approached the scene of the showdown. His troops were already in place, and all was in readiness: the only question now was, should he attack immediately, or wait for daylight to begin the assault?

The more Lee studied the situation, the more uneasy he felt.

One false move, he knew, and some of Brown's hostages would probably start dying. In an act of cautious prudence that was perfectly in character, Lee decided to hold off for the moment ... and to send a letter in to Brown and the other renegades who had shot their way into the armory.

Headquarters Harper's Ferry
October 18, 1859

Colonel Lee, United States Army, commanding the troops sent by the President of the United States to suppress the insurrection at this place, demands the surrender of the persons in the armory buildings.

If they will peaceably surrender themselves and restore the pillaged property, they shall be kept in safety to await the orders of the President. Colonel Lee represents to them, in all frankness, that it is impossible for them to escape; that the armory is surrounded on all sides by troops; and that if he is compelled to take them by force he cannot answer for their safety.

R.E. Lee
Colonel Commanding United States Troops.

By 3 a.m. the message had been passed on to Lieutenant Stuart, who was ordered to prepare to deliver it on command.

It was quiet along the river now; even the breeze had died off, as the mild October evening drew toward dawn. Pacing back and forth outside the armory with Stuart and several of his other commanders, Lee kept asking himself if he'd done the right thing, made the right decision.

What would happen if Brown replied to the offer with a harsh refusal—"No deal!"—and then immediately began to murder the hostages?

To guard against this possibility, the Colonel quickly drew up a set of contingency plans: at the first sign that the terms had been rejected, a hastily assembled "storming party" was to batter down the doors, then leap upon the rebels with bayonets. There would be no gunfire, insisted the ever-prudent Lee, in the hope of protecting the hostages from stray bullets.

It was a tense evening, to say the least.

At 7 a.m., and with the insurrectionists still holding firm inside the armory, the Colonel decided it was time to move.

He gave the signal.

While a crowd of about 2,000 amazed area residents looked on in awe, Stuart advanced slowly toward the doors of the armory.

Behind him, two dozen marksmen flexed their trigger fingers in anticipation.

Slowly, Stuart read Lee's terms to the grimy, carbine-waving John Brown—an outlaw whom Stuart easily recognized from his earlier years of keeping the peace as a federal trooper in Kansas.

But the crazed abolitionist hardly even listened to Lee's proposal. Instead, he chattered furiously, irrationally about extraneous matters … until the edgy Stuart backed away, sensing that his mission of diplomacy had proved fruitless.

At last Stuart signaled his men; in a flash, the assault of the armory was on.

It lasted exactly three minutes … and when the smoke cleared, four of Brown's men lay dead on the floor, while the rebel leader, himself, was bleeding copiously from a blow from a federal trooper's sword.

It was over.

And yet the firestorm of the abolitionist frenzy that had been triggered by Brown's "martyrdom" was only beginning.

Within a week or so, Lee would be ordered back to Harper's Ferry —this time to defend the armory against a feared assault by pro-abolitionist forces who had been whipped into insurrection by the pro-abolitionist press of the region.

Responding, Lee would direct the transfer of four companies of soldiers from Fort Monroe to Harpers Ferry, where Brown was scheduled to be hanged for his treason on December 2. That day came and went; in spite of widespread predictions to the contrary, there was no general uprising during or immediately after the execution.

It was history. As Douglas Southall Freeman would note later in his authoritative biography of Lee: "The day of Brown's execution passed without the appearance of any of the desperadoes who were supposed to be massing. Although Lee improved the idle time of the troops by drilling them in target practice, he and the men alike were glad when orders came on December 9 for a return on December 12 to their state.

"The country continued to debate bitterly the rights and the wrongs of Brown's attempt, but the affair seems to have affected Lee very little. 'The result,' he said in his report of October 19, 'proves that the plan was the attempt of a fanatic or madman.' He did not believe that the Negroes would respond to such appeals as Brown had made, and he troubled himself no more about it."

The accuracy of Freeman's description can be seen quite clearly in a letter Lee wrote to his Cousin Annette only three weeks after the capture of Brown at Harper's Ferry. In that brief message, Lee talks once again about his strong desire to "go down" to Cedar Grove ... and also about the warm affection he always felt for his cousin.

Arlington 8 Nov 1859

I shall want so much to see you tonight my beautiful Annette. for I know how sweet you will look, & of all those that will see you. none will appreciate the happiness as much as I would.

I have told Custis to look at you well for me & to tell me all about you. I was so sorry I could not see you as I came through Washington

Thursday. But you must call on your way home, & tell me all about the wedding, & how Miss Rosalie & Cousin Turb—deported themselves, & I will tell you all about Mary Childe & her man. You know she is a brave little woman.

I wish very much I could go down today. I do not think I would take up much space, or be much in the way, but your Cousin M—won't let me go—

You must remember me to your Uncle & Aunt & all around you, & give Miss Mary a kiss for me.

> *Very truly yours*
> *R.E. Lee*

Miss Annette Carter [15]

While Robert E. Lee did his best to enjoy every moment he could steal to be with his family, the growing tension between the Northern industrialists and the Southern aristocrats and farmers was already beginning to tear the nation asunder. And in the Old Line State of Maryland, where support for the South would remain strong throughout the approaching cataclysm, most citizens felt a natural alliance with the Confederacy.

And why not? Weren't both Maryland and Virginia dedicated believers in "States Rights"—the Constitutional principle that places fundamental political autonomy in the several states, and not in the central government to which they belong?

Indeed, that principle had always been honored in the North, as well as the South ... that is, until the industrial Northern states finally managed to gain a slight majority in the all-important House of Representatives. Suddenly, after that event, Northern insistence on the "power of the Union" flowered as if by magic.

As Lee knew, the Northern posture on this crucial question of States Rights was ludicrously transparent. Had not the New England states, themselves, threatened the dreaded "Secession" at their Hartford Convention, in order to demonstrate their powerful opposition to the War of 1812?

Lee listened to the swirling, ugly debate ... to the strident voices bellowing all around him. Then he turned away, rather sadly, to resume his duty. Like the others, he dimly perceived the outlines of the catastrophe that was coming; like many of the citizens around him, he already feared that the issue would end in blood.

Like so many around him, the dedicated military man simply did his best to get on with the business of living—in spite of the approaching storm on the horizon. Writing from Arlington to Ella Carter in the winter of 1860, Lee sounds a warm, domestic note, as he thanks her for a recent birthday gift; this revealing letter about "beautiful handkerchiefs" shows another side, the "family side" of the great military genius.

Arlington, Washington City P.O.
26 Janu. 1860

My dearest little Cousin,

I Cannot express my thanks for the beautiful handkerchiefs you have sent me. There is but one thing in your power to give, that I should have preferred & that is the sight of your sweet little self. You will know therefore how highly I appreciate your present.

I feel that I shall be the envy of all Texas, & fear that my vanity will overcome my repugnance to exhibit my treasures, for it will really be Casting pearls before Swine. They are beautiful & the embroidary has been so much admired that the petition to distribute has been universal.

I am greatly obliged to you my dear little Cousin but hope you do not think in this way to Console me for not seeing you again. You know you promised to Come up with Annette, & if you were to give me all Prince George, I should go Sorrowing to Texas, did I not see you.

I returned Tuesday from Richmond & found a houseful of girls, the Misses Fairfax of Alex., May Floyd, & Harriet Powell. It makes me the more anxious to See you & Annette. These eight spinsters have not induced Major A. to return to them & they are anxious to have him amongst them. Custis wants your aid to gratify them.

Tell Annette I saw Miss Holly Hasall & Bill Harrison in Richmond. They are not tired of weddings yet. Neither is the incomparable George. But I did not see Hilly-Lilly & Miss Jennifer was in Richmond.

I left Fitzhugh & Charlotte well. Both seemed pleased with their location, & the latter was as much engrossed with her house, as the former was with the farm. Such making of bread, Cake &–dishes: & sewing of napkins, table cloths you never saw. Their domestics were undergoing a rapid Course of instruction, as they had lately been elevated from the hoe & the plough, their astonishment & admiration were great. Uncle Williams was with them. They all made many inquires after you, Annette & sent their regards.

I should have many messages from the household, did they know I was writing, but I will leave them to write those themselves. I have not heard of Mildred returning to you. I hope she is well & with love to Annette & kind regards to your father I remain truly your

Cousin
R.E. Lee

Miss Ella Carter [16]

While Robert E. Lee tended to such family matters as writing thank-you notes to his beloved Ella, the gathering conflict over "Secession" was growing uglier by the hour, as Southerners everywhere —and especially in Maryland—prepared for the political cataclysm that now seemed inevitable. But what could the colonel of cavalry do, personally, to prevent the storm that was brewing?

Nothing. It was out of his hands. For Lee, "duty" had always been his response, when facing events that he couldn't control; once again, duty would be his friend. On the 10th of February, 1860, Lee would leave Arlington to begin the arduous journey back to his cavalry unit in Texas.

Before departing, he would pen a quick note to Cousin Annette at Goodwood, in which he expressed the hope that her grandmother, then living in Philadelphia, was enjoying good health.

(The grandmother was in fact Lee's half-sister, Lucy Grymes Lee Carter, and she was the daughter of Light-Horse and his first wife,

Matilda Lee. This venerable lady passed away in 1860, and although history does not record the month, the sad event probably occurred soon after this letter was composed.)

Lee wrote this letter at dawn, just before bidding farewell to his family and setting out on the long journey to Fort Mason, at San Antonio, where he would take up his next command.

Arlington 10 Feb 1860

My dearest Annette

The pain of leaving home is much enhanced by my inability to bid adieu to you, Ella & your father. I wished to go down & see you but heard of your father & Ella being called to Philadelphia & did not know where I should find you. I could only have staid one night, but that would have given me the opportunity of saying some of the many things I wished to tell you.

Why did you not come up & see us while your father was away? I want to see you so much. Won't you write me a little letter to "San Antonio Texas"?

My notice was very short—yesterday I rec'd my orders, & this morn'g I must take my departure. The Household is all asleep or I should have many messages to deliver—But the approach of day warns me I must take my breakfast & be off.

I hope your Grdmother has been relieved & that your father & Ella will soon be with you again—Remember me to them & to Mildred. God bless you all—I hope I may soon see you again.

In the meantime do not forget your Cousin.

R.E. Lee

Miss Annette Carter [17]

Any people whatever have a right to abolish the existing govern-
ment and form a new one that suits them better.

—Abraham Lincoln, 1847

By the fall of 1860, as the bitterly controversial Presidential election approached, the talk everywhere in Texas was of secession. Settling into the round of his duties at San Antonio, Lee did his best to
ignore the rising clamor in the South (and especially in Texas) among
citizens who felt certain that they were about to be betrayed by the
Northern industrialists who controlled Lincoln and his men.

Whether it was defending the Texas settlers against the occasional
Indian raiding party, or the more mundane task of conducting "spit
and polish" exercises with his cavalry unit, Lee worked hard to live
up to the Colonel's insignia he now wore.

By now, the record shows, the 53-year-old Lee was turning more
and more inward, as the outer world of men and their affairs continued to sadden him. Is it really surprising that one of his favorite lei-
sure-time activities was working as an "engineering volunteer" on the
construction of a new Episcopal Church for San Antonio?

While Lee was in Texas, his daughter Annie made one of the family's frequent visits to Goodwood, and her mother wrote to her.

Arlington, October 21, 1860

Miss Annie C. Lee
Care of C. H. Carter Esq.
Goodwood
near Queen Anne's Post Office
Prince George's County, Maryland

My Dear Annie,
I rec. a letter from Helen & will translate what she says for Ella's bene-
fit ... (she goes on to describe the price of bonnets and other clothing) ...

When is our Ella coming up to teach us the —— stitch?.
You must bring as many of the girls back with you. ... (7 page letter)

> *I am your*
> *affectionate Mother*
> *M.C. Lee*

> *Much love to all.* [18]

Writing to his son Rooney during this period, Lee sounds the re-signed note of a man who has learned to accept the limits of the physical world of daily events ... while also choosing to put his own faith in the "invisible" world of the spirit, and a prayerful reverence. "We want but little," he wrote to Rooney, who had just presented him with his first grandchild. "Our happiness depends upon our in-dependence, the success of our operations, prosperity of our plans, health, contentment, and the esteem of our friends."

In another letter to one of his sons, Lee concluded that life was hard for all, regardless of social position ... but especially hard on those who had the misfortune to inhabit the Southern States during the mid-19th Century. "The Southern states," he pointed out in a gloomy letter to Custis, "seem to be in a convulsion. ...

"My little personal troubles sink into insignificance when I con-template the condition of the country, and I feel as if I could easily lay down my life for its safety.

"But I also feel that would bring but little good."

Lee hung on. When duty called, he answered it. But when the news broke that Abe Lincoln had, indeed, been elected President—while winning fewer than 40 percent of the American vote (and only 2½ percent in Maryland)—the Virginia cavalryman knew that the hour of decision was close at hand.

From beginning to end, it had been a strife-torn, tumultuous elec-tion. First the Democratic Party's nominating convention, held in Baltimore that year, had exploded in raucous debate over States Rights.

Then, after the Northern Democrats picked Stephen Douglas as their nominee, the Southern delegates (the Marylanders among them, of course) had promptly bolted ... and just as promptly, had gone on to nominate the fiery John C. Breckinridge (then Vice President of the United States) as their hard-charging candidate.

With Tennessee's John Bell leading the Whigs and the former railroad lawyer, Abraham Lincoln, at the helm for the Republicans, the stage was set for an election that would shatter the tenuous peace of the Republic.

And when the results of the vote were tallied, crowds surged angrily through Southern streets.

Lincoln had won the election by sweeping some key sections of the industrial North—while garnering only a little more than one-third of the five million votes cast.

In Maryland, which Robert E. Lee had considered Virginia's sister state, the results were even more one-sided: While Breckinridge and Bell split 90 percent of the vote evenly and Douglas received about six percent, the newly elected 16th President of the United States had barely cracked two percent.

One other number shows the will of the people of Maryland in 1860 with stark clarity: In Anne Arundel, Calvert, Charles, St. Mary's and Prince George's Counties, where 7500 voters marked ballots that day, Abe Lincoln received a total of exactly 12 votes.

The results were immediate—and tragic.

In December of 1860, the legislature of South Carolina voted to secede from the United States.

In January, several other Southern states would follow suit.

Then, on January 16, 1861, Lee wrote one of the most interesting and revealing letters of his life. In a lengthy communique to "Cousin Annette of Goodwood," he made two basic points:

First: there no was doubt that Maryland belonged with the Confederacy, and would surely secede, along with the other states that were rapidly leaving the Union;

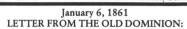

The Planters' Advocate

By THOMAS J. TURNER.   "TRUTH ALONE IS KNOWLEDGE—KNOWLEDGE IS POWER."   TWO DOLLARS PER ANNUM

Vol. 10.   UPPER MARLBOROUGH, MARYLAND, WEDNESDAY MORNING, JANUARY 16, 1861.   No. 22.

January 6, 1861
LETTER FROM THE OLD DOMINION:

Whatever may be our pride as to the former glory of the United States of America, and painful as may appear the reality, I think you will agree with me, that the fallacy of Republics, as the best form of government, has been most signally evidenced in the travalls of this land. We are rent asunder by ourselves, we are drifting to a Chavybodis that must forever blot out the glory and might of our name. The day has been when the demagogue, the partisan, the party ruler, would have been branded as the sole cause of our troubles, but these now slumber beneath the stormy waves of a great public opinion, and the masses of a free government –one that ought to have stood the test of time, and chimed its practical blessings to the latest generation – our people are plotting the instrument of their own destruction.

The question of Secession, heretofore considered and fearfully debated in the abstract, is about to make its mark on the page of history, as the overthrow of the Government of the United States. For one, I hail it as the Aurora that will rise and tinge the political sky of the great Southern Confederacy. I regard it as the last resort of freeman, who have used all fair and honorable means for an adjustment of difficulties with the North, and now take upon themselves to divide this Union peacefully, if possible –forcibly, if necessary. Our fathers never contemplated this government a consolidated one–they never entertained the idea of making a nation on themselves and posterity–aye, they even intended that the scale of policy should be evenly balanced, both North and South. They acknowledged the Sovereignty of the States in the simple fact of submitting the Constitution to the Convention of States, to be ratified –not to the whole American people in the aggregate, for then we would have been a nation and not a Federal Compact. Then, if we were independent, separate Sovereignties in 1789, do the grovelling -------- of this day pretend that this government can stay the march of Secession. The Constitution is a solemn covenant, equally bearing upon every State, and when its sanctity is invaded by State Legislatures, when on section actually abolishes our mutual guarantees in the Constitution, I ask if the league is not broken, if the cord that bound us is not cut in twain, and if we must not resume our reserved powers?.......

Could the Spirit of Calhoun rise from the grave, could the eloquent, patriotic Webster live again, or could the master mind of Clay once more return to earth, they would but see their verification of their own predictions –a government they loved, had indeed survived them but a few years. The spirit has departed, and the body longs to mingle with the sod.

The Planters Advocate
Upper Marlborough, Maryland
(Courtesy Maryland Historical Society)

Second, it was quite evident to Colonel Lee that in spite of his "great love" of the Union, honor and duty would both require him to defend his beloved Virginia first.

Soon after writing this amazing letter to Annette, Lee would resign his commission—while turning down an offer from Washington to become the military commander of the major army of the United States. He would then return to Virginia and volunteer to help the armed forces of the Confederacy in whatever way he could.

As the commanding general of the mighty Army of Northern Virginia during the next four years, Lee would enter the annals of legend.

To read this letter is to begin to understand why Lee felt that he had no choice.

Fort Mason, San Antonio P.O.
16 Jany 1861

The reception of your letter of the 18th Ulto: from Cedar Grove My Sweet Annette has given me great pleasure. It was very kind in you & Ada to think of me, & you must have felt that I was thinking of you & longing to see you.

I hope no young man accompanied the party of young ladies to Cedar Grove, in whom you & Ada took such delight, or I shall soon hear of you two being engaged as well as Ella Calvert.

I cannot however otherwise understand how the injury occurred to Ada's arm. I can nevertheless sympathize with her, for the other morn on dismounting from my horse, in attempting to give her a lump of sugar, she is as fond of Candy as a young girl, she got hold of my finger in her eagerness, & bit it severely.

It was owing to my awkwardness & not her fault, but still you can see I can write. I wonder if Ada's was owing to a bite?

I suspect that "Small package" you propose sending me is your sweet little self. You know you could send me nothing that would give me so

much pleasure. If it is, send it right off, & bundle up with it brightfaced
Ella. She will make it very little larger, & if you tell the Postmasters you
are coming to your Cousin, they will forward it with care & despatch.

But if it is not, it will be useless to send it, for it would not pass
through the P.O. of Queen Anne, before it would be taken and sent
to Billy Bowie, how then could it escape the cupidity of the Texans?

You must not risk it then, Annette, but keep it, & I will keep as a Xmas
gift your letter instead, which I prefer to any package except the one I
have mentioned. I was very glad to learn from your letter of the wellbeing
of all at Cedar Grove and Goodwood. I think of the occupants of both
very often & hope some day to see them again.

I may have the opportunity soon, for if the Union is dissolved, I shall
return to Virginia & share the fortune of my people. But before so great a
calamity befalls the Country, I hope all honourable means of maintaining
the Constitution, & the equal rights of the people will be first exhausted.

Tell your father he must not allow Maryland to be tacked on to S. Carolina before the just demands of the South have been fairly presented to
the North & rejected. Then if the rights guaranteed by the Constitution are
denied us, & the citizens of one portion of the Country are granted privi-
leges not extended to the other, we can with a clear Conscience separate.

I am for maintaining all our rights, not for abandoning all for the sake
of one. Our national rights, liberty at home & security abroad, our lands,
Navy, forts, dockyards, Arsenals & institutions of every kind. It will result
in war I know. Fierce & bloody war. But so will secession, for it is revolution & was at last, and cannot be otherwise, so we might as well look at it
in its true character.

There is a long message, Annette, for your father, & a grave one, which
I had not intended to put in my letter to you, but it is a subject upon
which my serious thoughts often turn, for as an American citizen I prize
my government & Country highly, & there is no sacrifice I am not willing
to make for their preservation save that of honour.

I trust there is wisdom, patriotism enough in the Country to save them,
for I cannot anticipate so great a calamity to the nation as a dissolution
of the Union.

But now I will turn to other matters. *What are you & Ella & Mildred & Mary doing? The latter is enjoying her school, I hear. Mildred was in Baltimore, & Ella I understand is as sweet as ever. You are all therefore in a happy State.*

You must give my love to all & be sure sometimes to think of your Cousin. He is as forlorn as he can be. Is surrounded by a parcel of men & hears of nothing but indians. But he is not going to tell you a word about either. There is a handsome young fellow here though. If I send him in for you will you Come? He wears an embroidered jacket with a black plume in his hat & a long sword by his side.

You would soften the aspect of this Country amazingly, which I confess is hard and uninviting, & if the troops are withdrawn from it, will soon be reoccupied by our red brethren. A Sergeant and 20 men from the Post above me recently followed a party of 25 nine days, who had been on a marauding expedition & punished them severely, killing 14, capturing 3 & 45 horses, their camp, etc., etc. They are constantly prowling around us & occasionally suffer severely. I arrived here a few days before Xmas. I do not know how long I shall remain at this spot but there are several others of the same sort within reach of me.

And now sweet Annette I will tell you goodbye, for there is nothing else here to tell you, as you will have already discovered, & will think of you always.

> Your cousin,
> R.E. Lee

Miss Annette Carter [19]

Robert E. Lee is the greatest soldier now living, and if he ever gets the opportunity, he will prove himself the greatest captain in history.
—General Winfield Scott, 1861.

It was surely one of the most somber—and one of the saddest —interviews ever to take place in Washington, D.C.

On a mild April morning in 1861, Robert E. Lee visited Blair House on Pennsylvania Avenue, in order to discuss his military future with a personal representative of President Lincoln, a former newspaper editor named Francis P. Blair.

Instructed by the President to "ascertain Lee's intentions and feelings," the diplomatic Blair was prepared to make Lee an offer he couldn't refuse: how would the U.S. Army Colonel like to serve as the commander of the new, 100,000-man army that was being raised to do battle with the Confederates?

Lee listened calmly. Only six days before (April 12), the angry Confederates had made a colossal mistake at Ft. Sumter, in South Carolina; hot-headed and frustrated, they'd allowed Lincoln to trick them into firing the first shots into the fort, after endless provocations by the federal soldiers stationed there.

Instantly, Lincoln had hurried to capitalize on this tactical error by the South; within a few days, the citizens of the North were being bombarded with patriotic speeches from politicians and newspaper writers and abolitionist preachers—all of whom were demanding that every able-bodied young man in the land should be quickly recruited, then hurried off to do battle with the "Rebs."

These eager new soldiers would need a brilliant commander: that was Francis Blair's message to Robert E. Lee. Would the Colonel—having been recalled from his cavalry duty on the Texas frontier in February—consider taking over the reins of Mr. Lincoln's army within the next few days?

As many historians would later point out, Lee had everything to gain by the move, and almost nothing to lose.

In his classic portrait of Lee, Pulitzer Prize winning historian Douglas Southall Freeman captures the moment perfectly ... while describing the agonizing choice that was forced upon a man who loved the Union, but who loved his native state of Virginia even more:

"Command of an army of 75,000, perhaps 100,000 men; opportunity to apply all he had learned in Mexico; the supreme ambition of a soldier realized; the full support of the government; many of his ablest comrades working with him; rank as a major general—all this may have surged through Lee's mind, but if so, only for an instant.

"Then his Virginia background and the mental discipline of years asserted themselves. He had said: 'If the Union is dissolved and the government disrupted, I shall return to my native state and share the miseries of my people and save in defence will draw my sword on none.'

"There he stood, and in that spirit, after listening to all Blair had to say, he made the fateful reply that is best given in his own simple account of the interview: 'I declined the offer he made me to take command of an army that was to be brought into the field, stating as candidly and as courteously as I could, that though opposed to secession and deprecating war, I could take no part in an invasion of the Southern States.'"

For Robert E. Lee, the die was cast.

Along with several members of former President James Buchanan's cabinet (Vice President Breckinridge, Secretary of War John B. Floyd, Treasury Secretary Howell Cobb and Interior Secretary Jacob Thompson), Lee would now withdraw from the Union he could no longer support.

His letter of resignation from the U.S. Army would be straight to the point, but something that he had hoped never to write.

Arlington, Virginia (Washington City P.O.)
20 April 1861

Hon. Simon Cameron
Secy of War
Sir:

I have the honor to tender the resignation of my commission as Colonel of the 1st Regt. of Cavalry.

Very resp'y Your Obedient Servant

R.E. Lee
Col. 1st Cav'y.

FAREWELL ADDRESSES OF THE SOUTHERN SENATORS

On Monday, the 21st instant, Senators Yules and Malloy of Florida, Clay and Fitzpatrick of Alabama and Davis of Mississippi, whose States have seceded from the Union took their final leave of the Senate in brief addresses. The following is the main portion of the remarks of the retiring Senators:

Mr. Jefferson Davis, of Mississippi, announced the secession of his State, and justified the set. He explained the difference between nullification and secession, and after stating that Mississippi had declared her independence, added:

"This is done with no hostility or any desire to injure any section of the country, nor even for our pecuniary benefit, but from the high and solid foundations of defending and protecting the rights that we have inherited, and transmitting them ----- to our posterity. I know I feel no hostility to you Senators here, and am sure there is not one of you, whatever may have been the sharp discussion between us, to whom I cannot now say in the presence of my God, I wish you well? And such is the feeling, I am sure, the people I represent. I therefore, feel I but express their desire when I say I hope and they hope for these powerful relations with you, though we must part, that may be mutually beneficial to us in the future. There will be peace if you will it, and you may bring disaster on every part of the country if you thee will have it. And if you will have it thus, we will invoke the God our Fathers, who delivered us from the paw of the lion, to protect us from the ravages of the bear, and thus, putting our trust in God and our own firm hearts and strong arms, we will vindicate and defend the rights we claim. In the course of my long career I have met with a great variety of men here, and there have been points of collision between us. Whatever of offense there has been to me, I leave here. I carry no hostile feelings away. Whatever of offense I have given, which has not been redressed, I am writing to say to Senators, in this hour of parting, I offer you my apology for anything I may have done in the Senate, and I go thus released from obligation, remembering no injury I received, and having. discharged what I deem the duty of man to offer the only operation at this hour for every injury I have ever inflicted."

As the Senators from Florida, Alabama, and Mississippi were about to retire from the Senate, all the Democratic Senators crowded around them and shook hands with them. ----, Hale and Cameron were the only Republican s_nators that did so.

The Planters Advocate
Upper Marlborough, Maryland
(*Courtesy Maryland Historical Society*)

Two days after penning that sorrowful note, Lee was summoned to Richmond and offered the command of the Virginia military.

The odds were long, and his heart was heavy. He was a 54-year-old grandfather, and he was already weary of the bloodshed, the violence that inevitably accompanied the military life.

But he was a man of duty, and the people who were asking him to serve were Virginians. Lee accepted.

Within a few weeks, the capital of the brand-new Confederate States of America would be moved from Montgomery to Richmond.

Lee went to work. While he labored feverishly to build the defenses of Richmond and the State of Virginia, his cousins across the Potomac were getting an up-close look at the meaning of political tyranny ... as President Lincoln garrisoned thousands of troops there —while also suspending the Constitutionally guaranteed right of habeus corpus—in order to prevent the Old Line State from joining the Confederacy.

Suddenly, the letters to Goodwood were interrupted, and the frequent visits to his delightful "Maryland family" were curtailed.

Already, their light-hearted laughter seemed eons away.

In the long, grim struggle that lay ahead, Robert E. Lee would be certain of only one thing: He would do his duty. And in the great darkness that was coming to the land he loved, that sense of duty would have to be his sun.

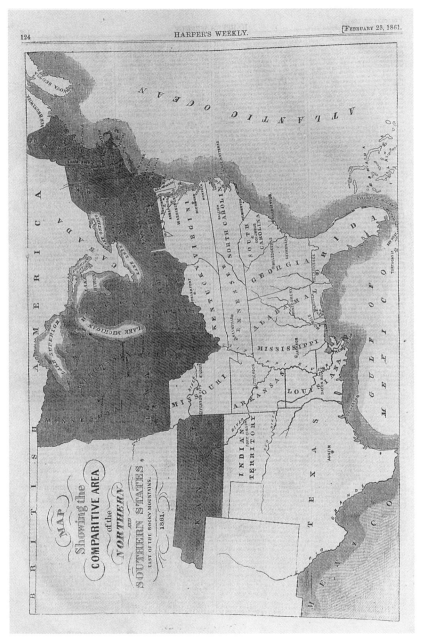

Harpers Weekly, February, 1861

CHAPTER FOUR

Seven Days of Hope

General Scott was consoled in a great measure by the reflection that he would have as his opponent a soldier worthy of every man's esteem, and one who would conduct the war upon the strictest rules of civilized warfare. There would be no outrages committed on private persons or property which he could prevent.

—Senator Reverdy Johnson (Maryland)

It was late April of 1861 before former U.S. Army Colonel Robert E. Lee arrived in Richmond—to the discovery that he had been unanimously appointed the "commander of the military and naval forces of Virginia" by the state legislature.

He promptly accepted, and then set about the business of establishing a Richmond office.

In a stirring speech before the Virginia Convention the next day, President John Janney told the world that the Old Dominion enjoyed the greatest confidence in Robert E. Lee, her native son:

"Sir, we have, by this unanimous vote, expressed our conviction that you are at this day, among the living citizens of Virginia, 'First in war.' We pray God most fervently that you may so conduct the operations committed to your charge, that it will soon be said of you, that you are 'first in peace,' and when that time comes you will have earned the still prouder distinction of being 'first in the hearts of your countrymen.' ..."

For the elected leaders and other notables who looked on that day, this eloquent phrasing must have seemed sadly ironic, as well as deeply moving—for President Janney was using the very words, to describe General Lee, that Lee's father (Revolutionary War hero "Light-Horse Harry" Lee) had employed at the funeral of George Washington!

But President Janney had not yet concluded his remarks, resuming: "Yesterday, your mother, Virginia, placed her sword in your hand upon the implied condition that we know you will keep to the letter and in spirit, that you will draw it only in her defense, and that you will fall with it in your hand rather than that the object for which it was placed there shall fail."

Lee nodded quietly, then returned to his duties. To say that he faced a formidable set of challenges at this very early stage of the war is to understate the matter entirely: the tasks he confronted now—to build and then supply a huge army, from scratch—made the fabled Labors of Hercules seem almost modest by comparison.

Recognizing that President Lincoln had vowed to begin his invasion of the South by May 5, Lee knew he had barely two weeks in which to begin shoring up Virginia's fragile defenses. His first priority: to defend vital Norfolk and its mighty seaport from the Federals, along with Harpers Ferry, where the gun-making machinery already in place might prove vital to the war effort. Almost overnight, Lee assigned large forces to begin improving these key areas.

At the same time, he was working frantically to create a chain of command and a general staff that could oversee the military forces of Virginia. With his former West Point aide, R.S. Garnett, safely on board, and with thousands of Virginians being mobilized daily, Lee and his assistants began to make inroads on the giant assignment that lay before them.

It would be a long, uphill battle to train and supply a brand-new army. Lee worked 18 hours a day, and demanded almost as much from his aides. Meanwhile, the fledgling Confederacy was doing its best to assist—by sending units to Virginia to help blunt the expected attacks by the Federals.

And those same attacks, to be sure, were not long in arriving. By May 24, the news broke all across Virginia: the Feds had occupied Alexandria and the Virginia side of the Potomac River.

Responding, Lee hurried reinforcements toward the key railroad junction at Manassas ... and did his best not to think about the fact that his beloved Arlington was now in the hands of the enemy. (Mrs. Lee quickly fled to temporary security at Ravensworth; later she would join her husband in Richmond.)

Meanwhile, President Jefferson Davis had arrived from Montgomery, Alabama; the new capital of the Confederate States of America had come with him. And one of his first moves—after lengthy consultation with General Lee—was to appoint a military commander for the Southern force that would defend the Manassas Junction: General P.G.T. Beauregard.

While their Virginia cousin worked diligently to build up the defenses of the Confederacy around Richmond, Charles Henry Carter and his Maryland kin were enduring the ravages of a political system that was bound and determined to prevent the Old Line State from accomplishing its own political will—a quick secession from the Union, and an even quicker application to join the budding Confederacy.

During the first few months of 1861, people all across the State of Maryland were calling on Governor Thomas Hicks to summon a special session of the legislature, so that the people's representatives could act on the clear wishes of the voters.

But Hicks, an unabashed Unionist, understood all too well that such a course of action would produce an overwhelming vote in favor of secession—and Hicks did his best to stall the issue until Federal troops could arrive.

And that's exactly what happened, on the 19th of April, when hundreds of Massachusetts regulars marched proudly through the streets of Baltimore ... in a display of Federal power that hardly struck a responsive chord among the pro-Southern residents of the Maryland city.

Utterly enraged, many of the latter began to hurl stones, while railing furiously against a President—Lincoln—who was in the midst of obliterating their own Constitutionally mandated civil rights.

The results were entirely predictable, and ghastly: when the smoke finally cleared, four Northern soldiers lay dead upon the pavement, along with 12 citizens of Baltimore.

Wherever you looked in Maryland, during that extraordinary springtime of 1861, influential leaders were stepping forward to defend the right of Maryland to leave the Union—and to bring her "just cause" to the open and waiting arms of the Confederacy.

In a particularly eloquent letter written in early May, a veteran Baltimore lawyer—Daniel Murray Thomas—whose immense knowledge of both the law and the government made him a widely respected figure in Maryland, predicted on paper that the "just cause" would eventually prevail.

Baltimore   4th May, 1861

My Dear Sister,

... After just two weeks, I have become a civilian again. (militia) Many persons are beginning to fear that Maryland has gone back again to the point she started from, but I don't think so.

People are too prone to despondency. We are doing all that can possibly be done under the circumstances, and while the paid mob are making a great show and talk, and thus scaring timid people into the belief that nothing can be done in Maryland, the real stamina of the State is working quietly and steadily the other way, and is strong because it does not choose to show its hand before the time for successful action arrives.

Our position is well understood at the South, and they don't expect us to do anything Quixotic.

Maryland will have to act with a great deal of tact for a time, but I am satisfied that a large majority of the people are with the South. The situation in the North is deplorable, and it should not be at all surprising if a state of anarchy is the result there. The immense number of troops raised there will not be amenable to civil pursuits. The decent men there will soon find that "the spirits they have raised abandoned them."

All this Marylanders must see very soon, and all will so see it much inclined toward casting in their lot with the more favored South. If we don't give up too soon to the North, the North will have to give up to us, and I say don't despair but be hopeful and in the end our just cause must triumph.

I hear Dr. McCabe has left West River in disgust. Is that so? Where are all the Union men now?

Yours affectionately,
Daniel Murray Thomas [20]

President Lincoln had seen enough: within days, he was pouring fresh troops into this renegade state, this hotbed of rebellion, and was arresting each and every government official whose loyalty to the Union cause was even slightly suspect. Suddenly, the right of "habeus corpus" had gone out the window, and the good residents of Maryland found themselves living under what most regarded as a "despicable tyrant."

In April, 1861 James Ryder Randall, a Marylander residing in New Orleans, read about the abuses in his home state and wrote a poem that was to become what Oliver Wendell Holmes would call the greatest war song of any nation and Maryland's state song.

The despot's heel is on thy shore,
    Maryland!
His touch is at thy temple door,
    Maryland!
Avenge the patiotic gore
That flecked the streets of Baltimore,
And be the battle queen of yore,
    Maryland! My Maryland!

Hark to a wand'ring son's appeal,
    Maryland!
My mother State! to thee I kneel,
    Maryland!
For life and death, for woe and weal,
Thy peerless chivalry reveal,
And gird thy beauteous limbs with steel,
    Maryland! My Maryland!

Thou wilt not cower in the dust,
    Maryland!
Thy beaming sword will never rust,
    Maryland!
Remember Carroll's sacred trust,
Remember Howard's warlike trust,—
And all thy slumberers with the just,
    Maryland! My Maryland!

Come! 'tis the red dawn of the day,
    Maryland!
Come with thy panoplied array,
    Maryland!
With Ringgold's spirit for the fray,
With Watson's blood at Monterey,
With fearless Lowe and dashing May,
    Maryland! My Maryland!

Come! for thy shield is bright and strong,
    Maryland!
Come! for thy dalliance does thee wrong,
    Maryland!
Come to thine own heroic throng,
That stalks with liberty along,
And gives a new Key to thy song,
    Maryland! My Maryland!

Dear Mother! burst the tyrant's chain,
    Maryland!
Virginia should not call in vain,
    Maryland!
She meets her sisters on the plain—
"Sic semper!" 'tis the proud refrain
That baffles minions back again,
    Maryland! My Maryland!

I see the blush upon thy cheek,
    Maryland!
But thou wast ever bravely meek,
    Maryland!
But lo! there surges forth a shriek
From hill to hill, from creek to creek—
Potomac calls to Chesapeake,
    Maryland! My Maryland!

Thou wilt not yield the Vandal toll,
    Maryland!
Thou wilt not crook to his control,
    Maryland!
Better the fire upon thee roll,
Better the blade, the shot, the bowl,
Than crucifixion of the soul,
    Maryland! My Maryland!

> I hear the distant thunder hum,
>   Maryland!
> The Old Line's bugle, fife, and drum,
>   Maryland!
> She is not dead, nor deaf, nor dumb—
> Huzza! she spurns the Northern scum!
> She breaths! she burns! she'll come! she'll come!
> Maryland! My Maryland!

One of the Marylanders arrested as a Confederate spy was Henry Brogden of Anne Arundel County. In 1863 he would find himself lanquishing in solitary confinement at Ft. McHenry under conditions so primitive that he would later write, *"At no times were the walls of my cell dry. Moisture trickled down it the whole time, and I could fill my hand with a green slime, simply by passing it up the face of the wall."* (This same Henry Brogden would marry Annette Carter in 1880.)

For Charles Henry Carter and the Carter clan at Goodwood, it was a betrayal that would never be forgotten: to this day, "true Marylanders" consider Abraham Lincoln to have been an opportunist who "sold out" the rights of the people for the sake of an immediate political gain.

Of course, many of these disaffected Marylanders weren't content to throw stones or jeer at parading federal troops. Intent on serving the Confederacy that owned their sympathies, they were streaming south by the thousands to join the brand-new army that Robert E. Lee was raising for the defense of Richmond, Norfolk, and indeed the entire Virginia Peninsula.

Two Southern Marylanders who went South were 21-year-old James McCaleb, who like thousands on both sides, died of Yellow Fever, and Henry Augustus Steuart, who immediately after the war began made his way to Virginia and joined the Black Horse Cavalry as a private. A hero at First Manassas, Steuart was promoted to Captain and assigned the extremely dangerous task of rounding up medical supplies and munitions in the Baltimore area, which was behind enemy lines.

The Planters' Advocate.

By THOMAS J. TURNER. | "TRUTH ALONE IS KNOWLEDGE—KNOWLEDGE IS POWER." | TWO DOLLARS PER ANNUM.
Vol. 10. | UPPER MARLBOROUGH, MARYLAND, WEDNESDAY MORNING, JUNE 12, 1861. | No. 48.

June 12, 1861
PROGRESS OF THE SECOND
WAR OF INDEPENDENCE
THE CONFEDERATE PLAN OF ATTACK

Some of the northern papers profess to have information to the effect that Jefferson Davis, Gen. Beauregard, and Gen. Lee have been in the consultation of Richmond for several days, during which they were in constant communication at Harper's Ferry. Gen. Lee, it is alleged, was eagerly in favor of aggressive action. He made a statement in detail, showing that there were 117,000 troops at different points in Virginia and 10,000 men in North Carolina were ready to march to any point in Virginia that their presence may be required. He advised an immediate Virginia attack on Washington and Alexandria by three corps d'armies of 25,000 men each, from Richmond, Lynchburg, Manassas Junction, Fredericksburg, Petersburg and Culpeper, and further urged an advance movement from Harper's Ferry on the Ohio and Pennsylvania troops. His views, however, did not prevail with the other generals, and it was finally decided by Gen. Davis and coincided in by Beauregard, to act entirely on the defensive, and that no troops were to cross the Potomac in any event. Harper's Ferry is to be held or abandoned as circumstances may demand. The line of railroad from Manassas Gap to Aquia Creek is to be the first basis of military operations, and will be defended by a force of 35,000 men, to be strengthened by an addition of 15,000 more if necessary.

The Planters Advocate
Upper Marlborough, Maryland
(Courtesy Maryland Historical Society)

But the daring Steuart didn't blink. With cool cunning he smuggled thousands of musket caps, fuses and other supplies past the Yankee sentries—until he was finally nabbed red-handed and flung into Washington's notorious Capitol Prison.

Yet this sudden imprisonment barely slowed the enterprising Steuart. Assisted by a couple of cellmates, he sawed through the bars of his cage. Then he bribed a guard with $50 and obtained a promise: if he survived the leap from the second-story window, the guard would look the other way while Steuart fled.

On the morning of May 11, 1862, Steuart prepared to make the leap. A voice outside shouted: "Come on!" Steuart yanked the sawed bars away, and climbed out on the ledge. In a flash, the bribed Yankee had betrayed him, shouting "Halt!" and firing off a round that struck the would-be escapee in the knee. He died later that day, after a last-ditch amputation failed to save him. Henry's father, William Frederick Steuart, Sr. (1816–1889), became so enraged at the murder of his son that he immediately headed south to join the Confederate forces. William Steuart would serve for nearly two years as a medical doctor for the Confederacy.

By late summer of 1861, it was quite obvious that the Yankee hopes for a "quick and easy" victory over the South would not be realized. The first real indication of that grim fact had come at the Battle of 1st Manassas, when Generals Johnston and Beauregard sent the Federals scampering back towards Washington City—many of them without their weapons, which had been tossed away in the panicked retreat.

Who can say what epochal events might have transpired, if only the Southerners had chased the fleeing Union mob back into the streets of the "other" nation's capital? But it didn't happen. Because the South failed to follow up on this huge victory, the North emerged with a new sense of anxiety and urgency about the war, while the South soon fell prey to a false sense of security that would cost her dearly.

Still, the Battle of 1st Manassas had been a smashing victory for

The Planters' Advocate.

By THOMAS J. TURNER. · "TRUTH ALONE IS KNOWLEDGE—KNOWLEDGE IS POWER" · TWO DOLLARS PER

Vol. 10. UPPER MARLBOROUGH, MARYLAND, WEDNESDAY MORNING, JULY 10, 1861.

July 17, 1861
THE BASTILE OF MARYLAND

Still the work of tyranny and oppression goes on in Maryland. Baltimore has its bastile, and its citizens are forced to submit to humiliations and wrongs which no subject of Francis Joseph of Austria, or of Alexandria of Russia endure. A Baltimore paper says, with an agony of shame and indignation:

"Under the arbitrary rule of a Massachusetts Abolitionist, our citizens are ruthlessly seized by the ruffian minions of his command, dragged from their homes and incarcerated in the cells of a fortress erected for their deliverance against a foreign enemy."

Is this the nineteenth century? Is this country America? —the land of Washington? —the spot made glorious in history by the brave battles successfully fought to establish the principles of freedom and self-government? Are we sure that we are not in the middle of the dark ages? Where is the man whose blood does not run through his veins like fire, burning his cheek with shame, at the thought of what deeds are done in the prostituted name of the "Union?" Sovereign States made this Union. Did they make it to become their jailor? Could the Convention of States that formed the Union have looked forward to the oppression and bloody events now transpiring, what State represented in its body would have remained a single moment to entertain the proposition for a Union? If our fathers, who shed their blood to achieve freedom, could have looked forward to see the use their degenerate sons would make of it, which man of all the brave army of the Revolution would not have thrown down his gun, and returned to the walks of peace? Behold the Chief of Police, and in fact nearly all municipal officers of the city, incarcerated in a military fort, charged with no crime whatever, and without the color of the law, at the arbitrary command of a mushroom general, who, five weeks ago, no more than the head of a counting room. Laws passed by the Sovereign State of Maryland are ignored by a Massachusetts Abolitionist, and the police of the city driven from their stations at the point of a bayonet, by the soldiers of Lincoln's army. The only hope left for us is that the conservative, anti-Seward force, yet remaining in the North, may be able to save the Republic from the disunion war schemes of the party in power. In the present Congress there is little to hope for. The limited number of brave and patriotic men in it will be powerless against the combined forces of the Abolitionists and the few traitor Democrats who have been bought up by Lincoln's war spoils –NEW YORK DAY BOOK.

The Planters Advocate
Upper Marlborough, Maryland
(*Courtesy Maryland Historical Society*)

"Johnny Reb"—whose triumphant force suffered only 1,981 casualties, compared to 2,646 for the badly shaken Union Army.

Lee missed that particular action, of course, since he had been engaged in other duties during the battle ... duties which later required him to make a visit to western Virginia, where he was doing his best to coordinate the struggle to control the mountains. But his efforts there would prove to be less than successful, and his frustration would only increase when one of his top aides (a great-nephew of George Washington) was killed in action.

Between November of 1861 and March of the following year, Lee would be on special assignment for President Davis, organizing coastal defenses around Charleston, South Carolina. And during his absence, the Southern fortunes would go into a down-spiral ... with the North piling up victory after victory in the west. Perhaps the worst of these setbacks was the one that took place in early April, 1862, when a Union general named Ulysses Grant led the Federals to a smashing victory at Shiloh, in Tennessee.

That two-day bloodbath, one of the deadliest in the history of the war, saw more than 23,000 men killed or wounded. And although the South suffered fewer casualties (nearly 3,000 fewer, in fact), there was no denying the obvious: the North could afford to lose soldiers in such numbers, day after day and month after month.

But that was not the case for the Confederacy; in a war of endless attrition, the Southerners would be wiped out long before their adversaries (a fact which became appallingly clear, three years later, in the desperate and blood-soaked "Wilderness" campaign south of Richmond).

It was a difficult time, to say the least. But by May of 1862, the Southern prospects had begun to improve. First, Stonewall Jackson launched his highly successful "Valley Campaign" along the Shenandoah. Next, General Joseph Johnston was doing his best in his campaign to block Union General George B. McClellan and his 120,000-man army from the approaches to Richmond—which by now ranked as a major prize, since it was the capital of the Confederacy.

The Planters' Advocate.

By THOMAS J. TURNER.   "TRUTH ALONE IS KNOWLEDGE—KNOWLEDGE IS POWER."   TWO DOLLARS PER ANNUM.

Vol. II.   UPPER MARLBOROUGH, MARYLAND, WEDNESDAY MORNING, AUGUST 7, 1861.   No. 2.

August 7, 1861
THE MARYLAND VOLUNTEERS

We have high praise awarded to the regiment of volunteers from Maryland, now serving in our army under General Johnston for their gallant bearing during the battle of Manassas. This regiment was, we learn, a part of the brigade under the Command of General Smith, whose timely appearance on the field when the struggle was the warmest, contributed much to determine the result of the fight.

All honor to those men, who, without awaiting the action of their own State, rushed to Virginia to manifest by their military services their devotion to States Rights, their love of Southern institutions, and their intolerable detestation of the Lincoln despotism.

But then fate stepped in. Badly wounded in the Battle of Seven Pines, the gritty Johnston was knocked out of action. Quickly, President Davis would tap Lee (June 1, 1862) for his new command.

As the Commanding General of the Army of Northern Virginia, Lee responded with an extraordinary display of military genius. Although badly outnumbered, he decided that he must break McClellan's grip on the terrain just north and east of the Southern capital, and thus end the Yankee threat to graceful old Richmond.

The result—known to history as the "Campaign of the Seven Days" —would make Robert E. Lee a hero throughout the South.

For he was the ablest general and to me seemed the greatest man I ever conversed with, and yet I have had the privilege of meeting Von Moltke and Prince Bismarck. General Lee was one of the few men who ever seriously impressed and awed me with their inherent greatness. ... His greatness made me humble and I never felt my own insignificance more keenly than I did in his presence. ... He was, indeed, a beautiful character, and of him it might truthfully be written: 'In righteousness did he judge and make war!'

—Field Marshall Viscount Wolseley

The Campaign of the Seven Days

Many years after the war, when the blood and smoke and thunder had faded, had given way to a melancholy sense of destiny—a sorrowful but obedient acceptance of "Divine Providence"—Lee would remember the crucial moments in the Seven Days Campaign ... would remember how for one shining hour, the possibility of completely routing McClellan's huge army had loomed before him, almost within his grasp.

Old soldiers never die! Sitting on the veranda of the President's House at Washington College in Lexington, and now a silver-haired grandfather, the retired general would have plenty of time to gaze off at the Blue Ridge Mountains he so loved, and to remember that glorious hour. ...

He could see them marching along the banks of the Chickahominy, marching toward Gaines's Mill, gray-clad, carrying their breechloaders at high-port ... and the drums banging furiously in the distance, and an excited voice was shouting *"We're moving up to Boatswain's Creek*—got McClellan on the run now, boys! Look smart ... here come the Texans!"

And then in memory he was patting Traveller's sweaty neck, and leaning forward in the saddle to shake Hood's hand. And the tall Texan grasping his own hand for a moment, squeezing it hard. And the dust whirling around the two of them—

It was 5:30 in the afternoon, June 27, 1862 ... and this meeting between the two brilliant generals, Robert E. Lee and John B. Hood, was one of the most hopeful and joyful moments Lee would experience during the early years of the war.

They'd met at the height of the Battle for Boatswain's Swamp, the key engagement that broke Union General George B. McClellan's grip on Richmond—and sent him staggering across the Chickahominy and then south toward the safety of his gunboats along the James River.

Slumbering in the chair, the older Lee could still feel the pressure of that hand. Could remember the immense weight on his own shoulders, as he struggled to find a way to drive McClellan and his 120,000 troopers from the outskirts of Richmond, lest the Unionists capture the capital of the Confederacy and end the war before it had even really begun. ...

Lee with only 57,000 soldiers of his own, but blessed with some of the most brilliant officers who would ever hoist a sword. Blessed with Longstreet, and Anderson, and Jackson, and Ewell, and A.P. Hill.

And Hood. Who was saluting him now, briskly and smartly, while the two horses bucked and pranced on the battle-scarred road that flanked Boatswain's Creek.

Lee, who had been in command of this Army of Northern Virginia for less than a month, returns the man's snappy greeting: "General Hood!"

"Sir?" The dust comes boiling up from the hooves of the Texan's steed.

"Can you break his line, General Hood?"

He meant McClellan, of course; for this one glimmering hour, the Confederates had the heart of the Union general's main force trapped, mired deep in Boatswain's Swamp. If only they could fight their way through the center of McClellan's line, smash his defenses, envelop him ... who could predict the future of the war, if McClellan were to be turned in a wholesale rout?

For a split second, the two military giants—the elegant, silver-bearded Virginian and the craggy-faced, scowling Texan—stared deep into each other's eyes.

"I will try," said Hood.

Then he was wheeling, their two horses plunging and snorting as a tremendous artillery burst ripped through the trees almost directly above their heads—

Gone.

What followed—the all-too-brief victory at Boatswain's Swamp, a major battle during the week-long series of engagements (June, 1862) that the historians describe as the "Campaign of the Seven Days"—was one of the most promising victories in the early part of the War for Southern Independence.

Because what followed that meeting on the swamp road was the rising, blood-freezing sound of the "Rebel Yell"—the battle cry sent up by General Hood's 4th Texas Brigade, as they joined Law and Pickett and Longstreet in a furious surge that brought them eyeball to eyeball with the center of McClellan's line.

Muskets barking furiously, and with the air sizzling and ripping around them, the inspired Southerners zoomed across the last 40 yards of mud-sucking swamp and plunged head-on into the Federal front line.

And suddenly, unbelievably, McClellan's bluecoats were flinging their breech-loaders aside, abandoning their heavy cannons and stacks of murderous grapeshot ... racing away in frantic, headlong flight from the raging Confederate juggernaut that was blasting their ranks to pieces.

On and on they went, the Texans in frantic pursuit: "Fire!" and the muskets crackled, spat orange flame, and "Fire!" and the line of re-treating blue jackets sagged, collapsed, rose again, and "Fire!" and everywhere that General Lee looked—from his perch on the knoll just north of the swamp—the story was the same: The Union line had broken! A complete route was only a few minutes away!

But it was not to be.

Although the great victory at Boatswain's Creek had broken McClellan's siege of Richmond, sending him reeling down the Chickahominy in headlong flight at the James River (and thus end-ing the Union threat against Richmond for at least two more years), the Campaign of the Seven Days would end in a costly vic-tory.

Lee had gained his first victory as Commander of the Army of Northern Virginia ... but the price had been terrible, indeed. With more than 17,000 dead and wounded, and with entire units deci-mated, the Southerners had taken a hit they could not afford.

Tactical victory ... followed by logistical and material defeat: What was the Seven Days, if not the entire history of the War for South-ern Independence, in miniature?

Brilliant tactics, and heroism in the ranks on a scale never before witnessed in warfare ... but with an accompanying loss of men and material that the Confederacy would never be able to sustain.

For one shining moment, everything had seemed possible. ...

Seven years later, sitting on that peaceful veranda at Lexington, the retired general would rehearse the campaign over and over again. Then dozing ...

Watch him jerk awake again. Rubbing his jaw. Coughing twice, and sighing his melancholy sigh. In the distance, a hoot owl calls from the treeline. Sitting on the porch and thinking it through for the thousandth time, and then concluding all over again: It was Providence, that's all.

--- • ---

In the decades to follow, the historians would write of the Seven Days that they had not materially altered the outcome of the war: short of a miracle, there was no way in which the South could have hoped to overcome the immense industrial and numerical superiority of the forces in Union blue.

But the confrontation between Lee and McClellan in late June of '62 certainly changed perceptions about the shape of the great struggle that was now beginning to unfold. There would be no sudden "lightning victory" for the North.

Suddenly, Lincoln and the Federals were confronting the grim prospect of years of unremitting, grinding warfare. And who could predict whether or not the patience of the civilian North would be exhausted before the issue could be won on the battlefield?

Describing the psychological legacy of the Seven Days, the American historian Allan Nevins summed it all up when he wrote:

"Before the North stretched the prospect of a prolonged war, with all its implications: dismaying financial problems, the necessity of conscription, a harsher scrutiny of Administration shortcomings, a deeper schism on war aims between moderates and radicals, rising discontent and disloyalty, a starker danger of foreign interventions.

"Until thus suddenly ringed by failure, most Northerners had hoped to see the insurrection suppressed without a profound national upheaval. Now revolution faced them on every hand: a party revolution as factional strife boiled up, an economic revolution as war contracts, tariffs and inflation spurred industry forward, a social revolution, even an intellectual revolution as millions began to think more responsibly and more nationally.

"From the beginning it had seemed likely that the war would mean the extirpation of slavery, the subordination of the South to the

North and West, and a business domination of government: now this was certainty."

Added Lee's most famous biographer, Douglas Southall Freeman, while describing the impact of the Seven Days on the future conduct of the war:

"The tangible results of the campaign were for every man's reckoning. The whole plan of Federal operations in Virginia had been disrupted after its success had seemed inevitable. On June 16 McClellan's army of 105,000 effectives had been like a sharpened sickle, ready to sweep over Richmond. Now it was crowded into an entrenched camp eighteen miles away.

"Fifty-two fine Federal guns were in Confederate hands. Ten thousand prisoners had been captured, and upwards of 31,000 needed small arms were gleaned from the fields. 'The siege of Richmond was raised,' Lee reported, 'and the objects of the campaign, which had been prosecuted after months of preparation at an enormous expenditure of men and money, completely frustrated.'

"Yet too many Confederate dead were buried between Mechanicsville and Malvern Hill, and too many men lay wretched in the hospitals for Lee to feel any elation. Of the 85,500 men with whom he had opened the campaign, 3286 were dead, 15,909 were wounded, and 946 were missing, a total of 20,141.

"Half the wounded, roughly, were doomed to die or to be permanently incapacitated for field duty. In other words, 11,000 men, the 'first line' of the South, had been lost to the Confederacy for all time. Federal losses were assumed to be higher, but actually they were less by 4,300.

"Lee had achieved less than he had hoped, less than he believed he should have accomplished. 'Under ordinary circumstances,' he stated in his report, 'the Federal army should have been destroyed.'"

June 25–July 1, 1862:	**The Seven Days Battles**
Casualties:	USA — 15,849
	CSA — 17,136

Lee and the Army of Northern Virginia had failed to deliver the knockout blow to McClellan and Co. And yet, for a while, events continued to unfold in favor of the Confederacy. Little more than a month after the Seven Days concluded, General Stonewall Jackson scored a rousing victory over General Nathaniel Banks at the Battle of Cedar Mountain.

On that same joyful day, Lee would write to his daughters Annie and Agnes, who were then taking shelter from the great storm in still-tranquil North Carolina:

"I received a note from Annette the other day by an unknown hand. From what she said I suppose it was one of her sweethearts coming to the wars. All was well at Goodwood. ..."

How sad it must have been, in the midst of this spreading carnage, to remember the mellow days at Goodwood—and the delightful Carter kin, of whom Lee had always been so fond.

But there was precious little time for such pleasant nostalgia. In the wake of the Seven Days, Lee understood very well that he must find a way to deliver a crushing blow to the North; such a quick, decisive victory was the only way to convince one of the great European powers to intervene and provide the South with desperately needed material assistance.

With this idea of a sudden, lethal strike at the Feds in mind, the crafty Lee set out to attack the new Federal general, John Pope, at Manassas. Then, in a stroke of supreme irony, Lee discovered that his own nephew, Louis Marshall, was fighting under Pope's flag.

Scornfully, Lee noted for the record: "I could forgive his fighting against us, but not his joining Pope." And there was a great deal of logic in Lee's scorn: He despised Pope for making war against civilian non-combatants. As a "gentleman soldier" of the old school, Lee had the greatest disdain for military leaders of the North, who saw warfare simply as a matter of destroying the enemy—regardless of the civilian casualties that were also caused by their undiscriminating gun fire.

And so it was with the greatest determination (and satisfaction) that Lee led his troops into the Second Battle of Manassas—a two-day slugfest that resulted in a resounding Confederate victory.

August 29–30:	**Second Battle of Manassas**
Casualties:	USA — 14,754
	CSA — 8,397

Describing the aftermath of the terrific beating that the Confederates handed the Federals at Second Manassas, historian Allan Nevins paints a vivid, appalling scene:

"On Sunday, under a cold, drizzling rain, Pope's dejected troops filed into the old Confederate defenses about Centreville. Behind them they left more than mounds of slain and wounded; they left all the bright hopes with which the Union forces five months earlier had begun their advance on Richmond.

"All the fatigue, the sickness in malarial swamps, the toils under burning Virginia suns, the endless fighting, the mutilations, the deaths of hosts of comrades, were in vain.

"They were back just where they had started, discouraged, cynical, resentful. They knew that they had been betrayed; they looked to the future with dark foreboding. At the best a deep melancholy, at the worst a bitter hatred of their incompetent leaders, possessed them; but their determination to fight on never flagged."

So much for the mood of the Union, in September of 1862.

But the South's stock had never been higher; in the brief, halcyon days that followed directly after Second Manassas, Southerners everywhere talked openly of "invading Washington" and "ending the war right then and there."

General Lee knew better than that, of course. Cautious, prudent by nature, he understood the terrible dangers that would accompany any attempt to meet the Feds head-on at the point of their greatest strength. But why not attempt a quick, punishing raid into the countryside of Maryland?

A sudden, smashing victory on what was technically "Union soil" might go far toward convincing the European powers that the Southern military owned the strength to prevail. And at the very least, a Maryland incursion would further inflame the vehement "peace party" in the North ... and lead to further wrangling over whether or not the war against the Confederacy should even be prosecuted.

Of course, Lee had one other reason for invading Maryland, even briefly: he knew that the vast majority of the citizens there deeply resented the tyrant Lincoln, and his cynical suspension of such civil rights as habeas corpus and freedom of the press, throughout the state.

By the first week of September, 1862, the stage was set for the invasion of Maryland—and for what would ultimately be the bloodiest day in the history of American warfare, as the Battle of Sharpsburg (also known as Antietam) exploded in an agony of unforgettable horror.

CHAPTER FIVE

Agony at Sharpsburg

From deep conviction I simply say this: A nation of men of Lee's calibre would be unconquerable in spirit and soul ...

—Dwight D. Eisenhower

The bands played "Maryland, My Maryland," and the soldiers cheered their lungs out.

On the afternoon of September 4, 1862, the first gray-clad columns of Lee's mighty Army of Northern Virginia came slogging through the knee-high waters of the Potomac and entered the Old Line State. What had been almost unthinkable a year before was now fact: the troops of the Confederacy, directed by General Robert E. Lee, were invading the United States of America.

After successfully fording the river—the crossing took place about halfway between Harper's Ferry and Washington—Lee's force made quickly for the small town of Frederick, where Southern sympathizers showered the soldiers with food and affection. And why not? Anyone who read Lee's "Proclamation to the People of Maryland," issued September 8th, could see that the Confederates intended to break Lincoln's tyrannical grip on a state that was clearly pro-Southern in sympathies, yet had been forced at gunpoint to stay in the Union.

To the People of Maryland:

It is right that you should know the purpose that has brought the army under my command within the limits of your state, so far as that purpose concerns yourselves.

The people of the Confederate States have long watched with the deepest sympathy the wrongs and outrages that have been inflicted upon the citizens of a Commonwealth allied to the states of the South by the strongest social, political and commercial ties.

They have seen, with profound indignation, their sister state deprived of every right, and reduced to the condition of a conquered province. Under the pretense of supporting the Constitution, but in violation of its most valuable provisions, your citizens have been arrested and imprisoned upon no charge and contrary to all forms of law.

The faithful and manly protest against this outrage made by the venerable and illustrious Marylanders—to whom in better days no citizen appealed for right in vain—was treated with scorn and contempt.

The government of your chief city has been usurped by armed strangers; your Legislature has been dissolved by the unlawful arrest of its members; freedom of the press and of speech have been suppressed; words have been declared offenses by an arbitrary desire of the Federal Executive, and citizens ordered to be tried by military commission for what they may dare to speak.

Believing that the people of Maryland possessed a spirit too lofty to submit to such a government, the people of the South have long wished to aid you in throwing off this foreign yoke, to enable you again to enjoy the inalienable rights of freemen, and restore independence and sovereignty to your state.

In obedience to this wish, our army has come among you and is prepared to assist you with the power of its arms in regaining the rights of which you have been despoiled. This, citizens of Maryland, is our mission, so far as you are concerned.

No constraint upon your free will is intended—no intimidation will be allowed. Within the limits of this army, at least, Marylanders shall once more enjoy their ancient freedom of thought and speech. We know no enemies among you, and will protect all of every opinion. It is for you to decide your destiny, freely and without restraint.

This army will respect your choice, whatever it may be; and, while the Southern people will rejoice to welcome you to your natural position among them, they will only welcome you when you come of your own free will.

R.E. Lee, General commanding

As this moving Proclamation suggests in every line, General Lee undoubtedly knew of the wide-ranging Federal repression that had come to Maryland with the arrival of Union troops during the previous year. He knew that many of the state's elected officials and civic leaders had been imprisoned because of their Southern sympathies—and were languishing behind bars at nearby Ft. McHenry, for no other crime than having an opinion.

He knew that outspoken newspapers such as the controversial "Planters Advocate" had been padlocked, and their editors hustled off to jail or forced to flee south. He understood that local elections were being routinely rigged, and that life in Maryland in the 1860's was no different than living in a foreign state.

Lee could feel the scorn with which many of the citizens of Baltimore and Annapolis and Frederick (and Goodwood!) responded to this rampant, Federal hypocrisy ... a double-standard in which Mr. Lincoln talked endlessly of "freedom" and "Constitutional rights" ... while violating the same, as Federal chief executive, each and every day of the week.

Undoubtedly, the great General was still receiving periodic letters from his Carter kin at Goodwood, during the weeks and months that preceded the showdown at Sharpsburg. Undoubtedly, he read their angry protests against a monstrously overgrown Federal government that had completely abandoned the Constitutional principle of "sovereignty of State."

Who is troubled, today, about the grotesque distortions that afflict our national life, in a world where the concepts of 1776—including the notion that power belongs to the several States, with the Federal government enjoying only those powers specifically granted it by the Constitution and Bill of Rights—were long ago sold out, then scrapped on the junk heap of history?

But Robert E. Lee was troubled ... troubled enough to lead his tens of thousands of gray-clad warriors across the ripe cornfields around Frederick, en route to a collision that would soon rank as the most costly in the history of American armed conflict.

Outnumbered almost two to one, the gritty Southerners understood that they were tempting destiny by crossing the Potomac and raising the Federal defenses of Washington. Knowing they were defending the capital, the men in blue would surely fight with brutal tenacity, and to the last soldier.

For Robert E. Lee, the stakes were enormously high. Because of the North's permanent advantage in men, industry and transport, Lee knew that he could not afford a sudden, devastating defeat from which his shattered army might never recover.

Indeed, the Virginia leader couldn't even afford a "draw." And the terrible difficulty of his position lay precisely in this: Lee had to win every time out, and win big. A mere "standoff" would only help the Yankees to slowly grind away precious Southern resources (in both men and material) until the Confederates were bled white and then defeated.

How could Lee strike at the heart of the Federal forces—for a quick, killing blow that might shock the world and bring support to the Southern cause from wavering Europe? From the very beginning, Lee had known it was their only chance.

And now, as he sat down to plan the desperate action that he knew lay ahead, several vital considerations loomed largest in his mind.

First of all, Lee knew that if he could just keep McClellan at arm's length around Sharpsburg, he would have time to resupply his straggling army from new lines that he'd opened back to Virginia. And if that step were accomplished, he could make a lightning-thrust westward to Hagerstown—a march of only a day or so—from which he could commandeer the trains of the Baltimore & Ohio Railroad for a rapid assault on Harrisburg, Pennsylvania, only 70 miles to the north.

Such a bold thrust into south-central Pennsylvania would allow him to take out the great railroad bridge on the Susquehanna River —thus separating the Union military machine in the western states from its allies in the East. And if *that* step could be achieved, McClellan and the other Union forces around Washington would be isolated ... might even be flushed from cover and into a battle where, with the Yankees for once deprived of superiority in numbers and material, Lee might inflict a devastating defeat.

Before taking Hagerstown, however, it would be necessary to knock out the big Federal garrisons at Harper's Ferry and Martinsburg, in order to secure the hold on the railroad and prevent Federal pursuit. Only then could the Pennsylvania attack begin.

It was a bold plan, and a remarkably risky one—since it required Lee to split his large force into five distinct units, each of which would be assigned a part of the task.

Exceedingly cunning in design, the plan to attack Harrisburg was vintage Robert E. Lee. It called for speed, deception, courage and decisive action—qualities which the Confederate troopers had always displayed in abundance.

Tragically for the South, however, the plan was not destined to succeed—and for a reason that defies both logic and understanding.

Somehow, an extra copy of the Lee battle plan (issued on September 9 and known formally as "Special Orders No. 191") was mislaid, and wound up being used as a wrapper for several cigars owned by a staff officer under Confederate General D.H. Hill.

In fact, however, the plans were found lying in tall grass by an obscure Union Army private and passed up the chain of command all the way to General McClellan ... who immediately began to brag that he would "whip Bobby Lee," and then dashed off a boastful telegram to President Lincoln:

"I have all the plans of the rebels, and will catch them in their own trap. ... Will send you trophies."

During the next few days, McLellan nearly succeeded in catching Lee's units in that "trap." Because he knew that the Southern force was split into several components, McClellan's decisions were easy to make: He could divide his own huge army (more than 70,000 troopers) into pursuing squadrons with impunity.

Suddenly, what had looked like a relatively easy assault on Harper's Ferry and Martinsburg became a much sterner test of Confederate will. And while General Lee's columns battled furiously to take the stubborn garrisons near the Potomac, his own position was becoming increasingly perilous.

Camped out on the flat corn and wheat fields along the crooked Antietam Creek—a narrow stream that wiggles south through Central Maryland to join the Potomac near Harper's Ferry—Lee and his men discovered with no small alarm that McClellan and Co. had somehow gotten wind of their plan to hit the railroad at Hagerstown. (And reportedly, it would only be after the war had ended, while reading Union reports about the Battle of Sharpsburg, that Lee would learn of the cigar-wrapped, intercepted plans.)

When the sun came up on September 17, it was clear to Lee and his aides that this would be a day of intense fighting. By then, the Feds had moved in so close that they were clearly visible along some of the ridgelines above the creek. And soon enough, the late summer skies above the Frederick County cornfields were blazing with the arrival of the first Union artillery shells, which began dropping into the Confederate lines at mid-morning.

It was to be a very long day, a day on which most of the major fighting would take place around the Dunker Church, Burnside's

Bridge, and West Wood—and along a Confederate-held sunken road that to this day is remembered as "Bloody Lane."

Because of McLellan's extraordinary stroke of good luck in discovering the mislaid plans, he was able to pin Lee down with a force that almost doubled that of his Confederate opponent.

The Southerners fought valiantly throughout the early afternoon, as the Federals sent attack after attack directly into the center of the Southern lines. And although each sally was repulsed—with ghastly losses on each side—the much thinner Confederate ranks were in terrible danger of collapsing. For a few brutally suspenseful hours, it seemed the entire Army of Northern Virginia, caught exposed around Antietam Creek and without any reserves whatsoever, might be annihilated.

For the brave men on both sides who struggled and bled that day, it was a scene to be remembered for the rest of their lives. In what was undoubtedly some of the most vicious "close-order" fighting that would take place during the entire war, Stonewall Jackson's stout-hearted brigade clashed furiously with the troopers commanded by the Union's "Fighting Joe" Hooker.

That gun battle—only one of many that would erupt throughout the day—saw men in gray firing head-on into the blue-clad ranks, frequently at distances of no more than 20 feet. Within minutes, the carnage was simply astounding; troopers on both sides reported later that the dead lay in huge, tangled heaps, their naked faces plastered into the mud. Meanwhile, on every quarter, soldiers half-insane with fear and rage stood firing and reloading, firing and reloading, while the cannons and the artillery roared around them like some great, iron-lunged beast intent on wholesale destruction.

Wrote one Union commander in the aftermath, when asked to describe what happened along the crooked little Maryland creek: "In less time than it takes to tell it, the ground was strewn with the bodies of the dead and wounded. ... Nearly two thousand men were disabled in a moment."

In the end, however, it came down to sheer will, sheer endurance. Having suffered attack after attack from the screaming bluecoats, the Confederate lines were unraveling everywhere, with company after company falling back in chaos and disarray. Again and again, General Lee was forced to deploy his ever-shrinking forces—with each new configuration of men and firepower more desperate than the last.

At the very last, all of Lee's chances would hinge on a single question: could he reinforce his center and right flank before it shattered entirely, triggering a catastrophic rout? And by 3 p.m., the answer to that question depended entirely on only four brigades—the 4,000 infantry troopers under the command of General A.P. Hill, who had been hurrying through a forced march from Harper's Ferry, 17 miles distant, which had finally fallen—at last, at last!—to the weary Southerners.

Could the hard-charging Hill get his fresh fighters into the battle in time to offset the chaos that had been caused by McClellan's huge superiority in artillery guns, and his two-to-one edge in infantry, during this long afternoon of ferocious assaults by the Federal marauders?

In an agony of suspense, Lee mounted his horse and rode out of Sharpsburg, toward an elevated knoll from which he hoped to be able to watch his army's desperate fate unfold. Frantically, he galloped west to a little wooded hill that might offer him a view of the decisive encounter.

At 3:30 on the afternoon of the 17th, Lee would endure the most critical—and brutally suspenseful—moment of the war so far.

Standing on the hill, he watched the endless plumes of smoke descending toward Antietam Creek, as the Union artillery rounds pounded the Southern troopers with ruthless fury.

Where was Hill?

Helpless, Lee listened to the shrieks of the wounded, the repeated roaring of the musket-volleys, the great tearing, earth-flinging explosions as the heavy mortar rounds went plunging into the Maryland cornfields. *Where was A.P. Hill?*

Suddenly, then, a column of artillery troopers was staggering past, lunging through the hellish smoke only a few feet from Lee's panting steed!

"Lieutenant!" the Southern Commander bellowed at the man who seemed to be leading this stunned mob of gunners, and who carried a supremely precious instrument—a telescope.

Now the man whirled, saluted, waited.

In a flash, the general was pointing toward a distant, rapidly approaching column. Could it be? *Where was A.P. Hill?* "Lieutenant —whose troops are those?"

Dazed and reeling, the Lieutenant struggled to focus the telescope. An agonizing ten seconds passed. Then: "They are flying the United States flag." Lee's heart sank; the bitter end of all his hopes now seemed inevitable. But then he looked up again ... and once again, a long column of arriving soldiers could be seen, outlined against the high ridges that flanked the blazing Antietam Creek.

"Lieutenant ... what troops are those?"

Again the lieutenant fought to bring the instrument into focus; again Lee could feel his heart nearly hammering out of his chest. For a moment everything slowed down ... way down ... and the smallest details stood out—a few green leaves, the last of the summer, dangling from a nearby black locust branch ... an abandoned military boot, its brown tongue grotesquely displayed, its long laces trailing in the mud—

"Sir!" the lieutenant was looking up from his telescope: "Sir, they are flying the Virginia and Confederate flags!"

It was Hill!

At the very last instant, they were saved!

And indeed, it was so: in what would later be remembered as one of the most valiant attacks of the war, General A.P. Hill and his foot-weary soldiers came thundering into view.

Bellowing and shrieking, the 4,000 troopers under Hill exploded into the Yankee lines like a runaway juggernaut. In every direction at once, the graycoats were firing, kneeling, rising, racing forward, then firing again ... and all the while roaring like a squadron of banshees just released from the depths of Hell.

Stunned—they'd had victory within their grasp!—the perplexed bluecoats began to falter ... staggered sideways ... fell back. Fell *back!* For the first time all day, it was the Northerners who were retreating; now it was the men in gray who pursued them over the muddy, rolling hillsides and through the corn stubble that gleamed fitfully in the expiring light along Bloody Lane.

When darkness came—when the long blue twilight of late summer finally came drifting and filtering down over this shattered, blasted landscape—two staggering facts were suddenly clear.

First, the cunning Lee, against all odds, had somehow escaped from McClellan's trap.

And second, this day of carnage had been unprecedented in the annals of American warfare.

The numbers tell us the ghastly story; they show that of the 110,000 men who fought that day, fully 20 percent—22,000—had been killed or wounded during the bloodbath along the creek.

Indeed, so vast was the tragic slaughter at Dunker Church and West Wood and Bloody Lane that it would take several days for the special burial teams from each army to accomplish their horrific chores.

In the end, Lee had failed to achieve his goal at Sharpsburg; his dream of a lightning-thrust at Harrisburg was over. After licking his wounds along the creek for two days, the Virginia general sadly concluded that a further offensive was impossible; his loss of men and supplies had simply been too great.

Under cover of darkness, the long gray lines began to ford the Potomac, headed back to the relative safety of the Old Dominion, where they could hope to rest, and recuperate, and heal their devastated bodies.

They would live to fight another day.

Sharpsburg, September 17, 1862. Battlefield on the day of battle. (Gardner) (*Courtesy Library of Congress*)

As for McClellan, the Federal commander: once again, the indecisive Yankee general would face withering criticism. Prudent, cautious to a fault, he had failed to pursue Lee's decimated forces back into Virginia, and within a few days, it was simply too late.

Lee had not been destroyed. But he had not gained the "great victory on Northern soil" that he so desperately needed, either. And so the issue remained in doubt, and no man could predict the future course of this war.

Still, General Robert E. Lee had managed to carry one great reward away from his blunted assault on the North.

Almost overnight, he had learned how to deploy a much smaller force against withering artillery and small arms fire ... while keeping his head and wringing the greatest possible advantage from every soldier and every gun in the field.

Lee had "gone to school" against McClellan at Sharpsburg, and if he was now a much more cunning, much more deliberate commander, it could mean only one thing: this great battle for Southern Independence was very far indeed from being over.

Describing the effect of the battle on Lee, Douglas Southall Freeman provides a remarkable insight: "The greatest development of the Maryland operations was in Lee himself. He did not abandon his view that the chief duty of the commanding general was performed when he brought the troops into position on the field of battle.

"He continued to leave the tactical details of action to the brigade and division commanders. But in the emergency of the day at Sharpsburg, when every general had been occupied on his own front, the larger tactical direction of the action had fallen to Lee and he had discharged it flawlessly.

"In a word, Sharpsburg was the first major battle that Lee had completely directed, and if he had ever believed, deep in his own heart, that his ability as a tactician was less than his skill as a strategist, Sharpsburg must have given him new confidence. For that action remains a model in the full employment of a small force for a defensive battle on the inner line."

September 17, 1862: **Battle of Sharpsburg**
Casualties: USA — 12,410
CSA — 10,318

Five years later this tragic day in Maryland would seem to have occurred not only in a different time, but in a different life, when General Lee would write his young niece Annette from Lexington.

Lexington, Va: 1 Nov 1867

My dearest Annette

I have just rec'd your letter of the 27th & you know the pleasure it has given me. Though I have been regretting your absence ever since you left, I am glad that you reached home comfortably & safely & found all well. I can readily understand how glad they were to have you back, but am at a loss to make you know how sorry we were to part with you & how much we regret your absence. My rides are entirely solitary now. Even "Traveler" seems to miss your enlivening presence & I fear is becoming as sombre as his master. But you promised to come & see us again. That is the only way to bring pleasure or to restore life to Lexington. Since you left, Capt. Henderson has not been to see us, but takes long walks with Custis. What he imparts to him may be numbered among the secrets of the grave, while I talk to Traveler, & feel equally sure of his discretion. I shall be anxious to receive your picture, but he must be a skilful artist to paint you as I know you, or to equal the portrait that I have constantly before me.

I am very much obliged to you for the cravat. I hope it will last forever, & it certainly will if it lasts as long as my admiration. But do not think that it is necessary to recall you to my thoughts for you live there always, & I cherish the hope of being able to get to Goodwood to see you all once again. You had better make up your mind to marry Custis & come & live with me always. He is so poor that you will not be tempted into any extravagance. I suppose pretty Mary Carter is full of her finery. Tell her she might as well spare herself the trouble. Major B. will not see a piece of it.

We have had three brides here since your departure. They all go down to the Natural bridge, which possesses for me more attractions since I have visited it with you.

We are expecting a visit from Fitzhugh daily. He is to be married on the 28th of this month, & says he cannot think of its taking place unless I'm present. This is a sore trouble to me for I had not intended to attend. My going will not only be an inconvenience to myself but to others, & then I shall have to see so many persons that I will be unable to see those I desire. When I go to Goodwood, Annette, you may be sure that I go to see you, your father & sisters & their families, & that you must be with me wherever I go.

... Now Sweet Annette I must bid you farewell, but I hope not for a long time, for you must write to your Uncle who loves you so dearly, & do not be deterred by his tedious letters. If he wrote forever he could not tell you how dear you were to him. Most truly & affectly yours

R.E. Lee [21]

How differently Lee would think of Maryland in 1867 than he had in September of 1862!

CHAPTER SIX

·

The Confederate Tide Surges On- Fredericksburg & Chancellorsville

·

No war in history was a more sincere conflict. It was not a war for conquest or glory, to call it rebellion is to speak ignorantly; to call it treason is to add viciousness to stupidity. It was a war of ideas, political conceptions and of loyalty to ancient ideals of English freedom.

—United Confederate Veterans

Sharpsburg was behind him now, nothing more than a bad memory, and Lee's Army of Northern Virginia had escaped from what might have been a crushing disaster at the hands of General George B. McClellan's vastly superior force. Now there was time—as the mellow autumn days deepened slowly into the first sharp frosts of October—to pause for a few weeks, to allow his exhausted troopers to heal and refresh their battered bodies ... and to try to weigh the costs of the standoff at Antietam Creek.

Lee knew that his army had been mauled terribly at Sharpsburg, and that he couldn't afford to continue trading manpower and material "even-up" with an enemy who had limitless resources. Already, he was dreaming of the next invasion of Maryland, the next assault on Pennsylvania. And why not? Wasn't it the South's only chance?

Sooner or later, the Confederates had to "win big" on Northern soil, in the desperate hope that a credible invasion above the Mason-Dixon Line would sway the Europeans and further disillusion the already disgruntled "Peace Party" of the North.

He must invade! But it was impossible; each time General Lee moved among his bivouacking troops in their hastily erected tent camps along the Rappahannock, their plight became more obvious: these men were half-dead with war fatigue. They lacked clothing, blankets, bullets, shoes. They were ragged skeletons, underfed and shivering, wrapping themselves in torn flour sacks and moth-eaten bedclothes, and wearing leaky cardboard shoes stuffed with news-paper.

He must be patient. He must *work*. In a furious effort that left him utterly spent each evening, he labored to re-supply the men in gray ... sent out appeal after appeal, until at last the supply-wagons full of boots and trousers and winter coats were lined up ten deep at every depot. And it was the same story with their rations: Lee spared no expense, buying entire herds of cattle from passing drov-ers, and authorizing the purchase of tons of other desperately need-ed foods: bread, rice, fresh vegetables, coffee, sugar, and mountain loads of fresh apples and peaches from the great orchards of the Shen-andoah Valley.

Camped outside Warrenton by late October, the General watched his 75,000 warriors growing stronger by the day, as their battered feet healed inside brand-new boots and their bellies expanded under huge helpings of the nightly, savory stew.

Sharpsburg had cost him dearly, there was no denying that. The Federals had scored a slashing body blow to the Army of Northern Virginia, and President Lincoln had poured salt into that wound a few days later (Sept. 23, 1862) with his "Emancipation Proclamation," which announced that all slaves would be freed by the following

January 1 ... but only in those districts where the people were "in rebellion against the United States."

Of course, the real motivation behind the "Emancipation" had little to do with the "plight of the Negro." In fact, many Northerners had kept slaves during the Colonial era, and a few still did; there had been very little outcry against the practice in the North. No, the actual purpose of the "Proclamation"—even if disguised behind high-minded, noble rhetoric—was to make it difficult for any of the European powers to come to the aid of the South.

Suddenly, now that Lincoln had decreed that the practice be ended, any government that assisted the South with supplies—or even with soldiers—would be supporting a "slave state" against a government that had declared the practice morally indefensible.

For Lincoln and the politicians of the North, the Emancipation Proclamation was a triumph of "public relations"—and so what if it was short on substance, and long on noble sentiments and easy promises? In the end, the document would serve its purpose; the European powers would be kept out of the war, in spite of the great admiration that many of them felt for the Southern cause.

For Lee and the South, this would be the greatest tragedy of all: the failure of the English, especially, to step forward with assistance ... even though the people of the British Isles were openly admiring of the cunning resistance that Lee's outmanned squadrons were offering, while remaining openly skeptical of the Yankee hordes of industrialists, contractors, suppliers and others who were "making a fortune" out of the war.

During the autumn of 1862, the British press was full of such praiseful news stories and editorials about the "cunning generals" of the "valiant South." But these were only words—and unless they sufficed to convince Queen Victoria's ministers to intervene militarily, such high-flown journalism was of no use to Lee.

Still, he could hope.

And during this six-week period of recuperation along the Rappahannock, hope was all Lee had. While he waited for his soldiers to

THE SITUATION IN AMERICA
August 30, 1862

The time seems to have come at last when the Federal Government, slow to believe and slow to act, is prepared to recognise the stupendous nature of the work it has commenced in combatting by force of arms the determination of the Southern States to maintain their independence. The Northern people, impelled by passion and not by reason— for reason would have allowed the South to go in peace as soon as it became evident that their fellow Southern-fellow citizens were earnest and unanimous in their desire to secede. Mr. Lincoln, his Cabinet, the press, the New England population, and all the large class of contractors, sutlers, and others, who are making rapid and scandalous fortunes out of the war, have decided within the last few weeks that the fight has not hitherto been fought as if the whole heart and purpose of the people and the Government were in it, and that it is necessary to carry on hostilities against their countrymen in as vigorous and unmerciful a spirit as if they were foreign foes leagued for the invasion of their soil and destruction of their liberties........In fact, much as the North hates disunion, it hates negro emancipation still more.....New England may call lustily for the abolition of negro slavery; but the Northern, the Middle, and the great Western States repudiate the political partnership, would fight to the death against the social equality.

SEPTEMBER 20, 1862

The Confederate Generals have shown themselves eminently vigilant and energetic, prompt to take advantage of every weakness or oversight or mistake of the enemy to which they have been opposed; they have cooperated with each other with almost mechanical exactness; and they have evidently been pursuing a plan of operations which was probably devised by some mastermind.

London News, 1862

heal and his supplies to arrive and his "stragglers" to be rounded up, he was hearing daily reports of the huge force McClellan was continuing to assemble for the Army of the Potomac, which now numbered more than 120,000 men.

"He's biding his time," Lee's spies reported again and again. "He's putting together an army so large that when he's ready, he can simply overwhelm you, wear you down through attrition."

Lee paced, and fretted, and watched the swirling, mud-yellow waters of the Rappahannock carry the last of the autumn leaves past his headquarters-tent at Falling Waters, located near Warrenton in the foothills of the Blue Ridge. Bending over a table covered with maps, or sitting in endless meetings with his weary commanders, he struggled to keep his concentration focused, his eye on the target.

For in truth, the General was heartsick, was deeply frightened about a new development in his own family: his beloved Annie, his 23-year-old daughter and the apple of his eye, had fallen grievously ill with typhoid fever.

By early October, Mrs. Lee was on the road to Jones Springs, North Carolina—thank God Cousin Ella Carter had been able to accompany her!—where she would join Annie's sister, Agnes, in caring for the invalid. How serious was her condition? Extremely serious, apparently ... or so it seemed, from the tone of the letter Agnes wrote to her sister Mildred, early in the month: *"Annie continues the same, very tired & her fever still unbroken. Ella, Ma, and I keep up our nursing."*

While Lee paced back and forth along the muddy tent rows, gnawed with worry about his ailing daughter, the struggle to keep Annie alive was growing more desperate with each hour.

By the end of the first week of October, Annie's chills had deepened into chronic fever and intestinal discomfort. Was it only the flu? No ... within a few days, her raging fever and growing weakness alarmed the entire family. Soon the local doctor was summoned; he took one look at her rash and dark red tongue and made the ghastly diagnosis: it was typhoid.

Soon poor Annie's temperature was soaring to 106 degrees, and she seemed perilously close to falling into a coma. With Agnes, Ella and Mrs. Lee taking turns as nurses, the entire family waited in dreadful suspense for the final twist of the knife.

It soon arrived.

"Annie [is] much worse than when I came," Mrs. Lee reported to Mary Custis, *"more attenuated and pulse higher. The disease must be at its crisis now. She has been suffering today with pain in her stomach and bowels. She is so deaf she can scarcely hear a word."*

A few hours later, she added a truly alarming postscript: *"Annie passed a very uncomfortable night; the doctor considers her extremely ill."*

And indeed, it was so; now the young woman lay helpless in the coma they had all dreaded. Suddenly she roused herself, and asked to see a hymn book; for a moment, their spirits rose.

But she was too weak to read the words.

Slowly, the collection of sacred songs toppled from her inert fingers. ... *"Mama thinks her hand rested on a hymn entitled 'In Extremity,'"* Agnes would write to Mary Custis later. *"That night she said, 'Lay me down; lay me down, and afterwards I am ready to rise,' which I feel now referred to what was to come."* 22

At 3 o'clock on the morning of October 20, Annie cried out: "Where is Agnes? Help me!"

Fighting back her own tears, Agnes held her close and tried to soothe her.

Four hours later, Annie took a few quiet, peaceful breaths ... and finally expired.

When the news reached Robert E. Lee on the battlefield of Virginia, he did his best to control his feelings. *"God has taken the purest and the best,"* he would write later to his son Custis, *"but His will be done."*

Still, it was an agonizing acceptance. And how unnatural, for a child to die before her parents! Surrounded by the death and destruction of warfare, and witnessing every hour the bestial violence of

Mary Custis Lee (Mrs. Robert E. Lee), Ella Carter, Agnes Lee attending to the dying Annie Lee, North Carolina, 1862

man's inhumanity to man, Lee struggled against the swirling despair that torments all of us in hours of grievous loss.

The pathos of Lee's situation must have seem poignantly clear to his aide, Major Walter Taylor, who one afternoon made the mistake of entering the General's tent unannounced.

Stunned, Taylor confronted a man with his head in his hands: the great Robert E. Lee, who had just learned of Annie's demise, was weeping his heart out.

His will be done!

Lee cried, and stared out at the lapping Rappahannock, and struggled to accept his fate. And then—incomparable man of duty that he was—he dragged himself back to the table, back to the military maps.

For a great, history-making battle loomed directly ahead, and its name would be Fredericksburg.

On the tenth of November, 1862, with the huge Federal army having crossed the Potomac and apparently making for the line of Lee's defenses along the Rappahannock, there was a startling development: the Virginian's longtime adversary, George B. McClellan, had been replaced at the helm of the Army of the Potomac!

"We always understood each other so well," Lee would ruefully tell an aide, before settling in to study the temperament and tactics of McClellan's replacement, Major General Ambrose E. Burnside.

The first question Lee faced, in attempting to analyze Lincoln's sudden switch in commanders, was whether or not the new leader also carried a new battle plan. Until now, Lee had mapped out every movement of his troops with one key idea in mind: *At all costs, protect Richmond!* Nor had there had ever been any doubt in Lee's mind that, sooner or later, McLellan would return to his original dream of taking Richmond in a fullscale, smashing assault that would leave the entire Confederacy in tatters.

But Burnside appeared to be cut from different cloth; instead of grinding directly south toward the Confederate capital, regardless of his losses, he had veered off to the west, toward the placid and tranquil little town of Fredericksburg, where by November 20 his heavy guns and his mortar batteries were already digging into the hillsides above the Rappahannock.

And indeed, you didn't have to be a military genius to understand that a major engagement was looming here: by the afternoon of the 22nd, while a cold, heavy rain slanted into the oaks and maples above Aquia Creek and the North Anna, the streets leading out of Fredericksburg were swarming with loaded-down civilians—women and children, mostly—who carried their household furnishings and their precious clothing upon their backs.

Watching that sad, rainswept procession, Lee would feel an immense empathy for these ordinary Virginians, many of whom would never see their homes again. "History presents no instance," he would remark years later, while remembering the hours that led up to this great Southern victory, "of a people exhibiting a purer and more unselfish patriotism, or a higher spirit of fortitude and courage than was evinced by the citizens of Fredericksburg.

"They cheerfully incurred great hardships and privations, and surrendered their homes and property to destruction rather than yield them into the hands of the enemies of their country."

Marveling at their courage, Lee waited for the great bombardment to begin.

But one day passed ... and then another ... and then five. And nothing. What in the world was Burnside up to? Was this sideways swipe along the river nothing more than a feint? Would the Yankee commander suddenly pull out of his encampments beside the water and run for Richmond?

No. It couldn't be. Burnside was too dug in; it would be too difficult. The target *had* to be Fredericksburg; there was no getting around it; every other scenario was simply too unlikely, too daring for the cautious Yankee general. ...

Warily, uneasily, Lee ordered Stonewall Jackson's brigade to nudge in closer on his flank, providing crucial reserves. And Stonewall responded: by the first of December, his fearsome troops were striding out of the Shenandoah—ankle-deep now, in winter's first snow—

and taking up their positions above the railroad bridges and the two highways that led into Fredericksburg.

They were ready.

And yet, incredibly, nothing happened.

Ten more days passed ... gray, wet mornings full of fog and sleet ... pale afternoons, when the wind came slanting out of the distant Blue Ridge to gnaw and nip at the shivering men ... black nights full of barking dogs and whirling snow. Why didn't Burnside move? Why were the Yankee guns still silent? When would the great dark snouts of the heavy cannons begin to flash with the demon's fire?

At dawn on the 11th, the Confederate pickets along the outskirts of Fredericksburg strained to see through a rising, swirling mist. What ghostly forms were these, hovering along the edge of the running water? Leaning forward on their horses, the sentries strained their eyes ... went half-blind in the effort to pick out the forms moving toward them, to identify these loping shadows—

It was the engineers!

The Federal engineers were zooming along the water's edge, laying in the first stages of the pontoon bridges that the troops would have to cross, later that day!

It had begun.

Now the pickets whirled on their horses, spurred them, galloped toward Lee's command post in the nearby town. "Pontoon bridges, sir—the engineers are already laying them in!"

Within a few hours, the Federals would launch one of the major artillery bombardments of the war ... a roaring firestorm of flying lead that would leave the screaming women and children who had remained behind huddled in their basements, hands covering their ears, praying desperately for this Yankee-orchestrated nightmare to end.

While two huge Federal hot-air balloons directed the action from overhead, a hundred Union artillery pieces poured at least 5,000 screaming shells into the battered collection of woodframe houses that lay in the shadow of Stafford Heights. From Hunter's Island at one end of town to the rippling waters of Hazel Run at the other, this elegant old river town was slowly coming apart at the seams.

But the Confederate marksmen—many of them crack riflemen from Mississippi—would not surrender the town without a blistering fight. All day long, against three to one odds, the marksmen held their ground, ignored the crashing artillery rounds, and picked off the bluecoats one by one.

And it was long after dark when they finally acted on their orders from General Lee: *Abandon the city proper; fall back to positions at Marye's Heights.*

Throughout the following day, the 12th, both sides jockeyed for position. But Lee did manage to accomplish one key step: around noon, he reconnoitred the Yankee lines, accompanied by General Stonewall Jackson, and moved in so close to the advancing Union troops (three or four hundred yards) that he could actually read their expressions through his field glasses.

There was no more doubt: Burnside had chosen to fight here, now, at Fredericksburg!

The 13th day of December—the major day of the battle—began with a thick, yellowish fog drifting along the sluggish Rappahannock, as if the gods, themselves, didn't want to witness the carnage that was coming.

As always, the numbers were stacked solidly against Lee; while General Burnside could count on deploying more than 125,000 bluecoats during the next few hours, the Confederates had been able to assemble no more than 78,000.

By ten o'clock in the morning, the fog had begun to lift; already, the first Federal batteries were barking and stuttering, kicking black smoke, as the shells went slamming into the Southern ranks. An hour later, the Union infantrymen were churning into their first attack against A.P. Hill's stalwarts—and within half an hour, they had been thrown back upon themselves, with the assault completely blunted.

Even as the tigerish Hill raked the Yankee foot-soldiers with a few blasts from his own artillery, Southern General James Longstreet was peppering the bridges at the far end of town with his pesky 30-pounders. That wouldn't stop the Yankees, of course, in their quest to take Marye's Heights, and the command posts of the Confederate Army … but it would certainly slow them down, while Lee and Co. did their best to brace the grayclads against the uphill assault that Burnside was preparing.

Just before noon, Burnside made his move, and it turned out to be a foolish one. In spite of the fact that the Confederates were swarming along the "Sunken Road" and firmly dug in on the side of the hill behind a wall, Burnside decided to assault Marye's Heights with thousands of troops.

Such thoughtless positioning left the bluecoats completely exposed to withering Southern fire from above.

Yet that was precisely the strategy that Burnside employed.

The first surging rush of the Yankee foot soldiers exploded up the hill. For a hundred yards the stumbling troopers lurched forward, firing at will, but the thrust could not possibly succeed … not with the Confederate artillery gunners ripping huge swaths in the Union ranks, virtually at will. Shattered, ripped to bleeding pieces, the Union force fell back toward its defensive position: the Rebel line had held!

But there was little time to waste on celebration; within an hour, the Feds were once again rolling forward, intent on a high-speed collision with Lee's right flank. But once again, the Confederate artillery ruled the skies; everywhere you looked the Union blue was reeling in confusion, staggering for a moment, then toppling to the blood-soaked earth.

Lee, watching all of this from an elevated spot above the town (an area known ever since as "Lee's Hill"), paced anxiously from one messenger to the next: Where was Jackson's brigade? Was A.P. Hill in trouble? If not, why had his gray-suited battlers vanished from the thick "neck" of forestland that flanked Marye's Heights—to be replaced by cheering Union soldiers, for half an hour or so?

The fog of war! In the blowing smoke of the guns, in the roaring and bellowing of red-hot iron and the screams of the wounded, nothing could be known for sure. And for a terrible hour or two, it seemed that Lee's ranks would crack ... that Longstreet and Jackson and Hill would prove unequal to the task, outnumbered as they were.

Then, somewhere in mid-afternoon, the hills above Fredericksburg began to echo with a rising, siren-like wailing ... an unearthly howling that raised the hair on your neck and left the commanders on the Heights straining to see what new event had suddenly transpired to bring on this vast, spreading "Rebel Yell."

It was a Confederate countercharge, along the entire line of battle, and the Rebels had the bluecoats on the run!

Could it be?

Yes ... it could. It was. In every direction at once, now, the panicked Northerners were breaking ranks, throwing down their weapons, fleeing before the Confederates like a school of panicked minnows racing before a yawning shark. And on the Southerners came, still shrieking, throwing their voices before them in what had now become a streaming, wholesale rout!

Unable to believe his eye, Lee whirled to Longstreet, and made a remark that would become part of his legend: "It is well that war is so terrible—we should grow too fond of it!"

But Burnside would not give up.

By twilight, he had managed to re-gather his rattled forces, reorganize his faltering brigades. And once again, defying all logic and common sense, he ordered a mighty charge of horses and men. And once again, the withering artillery fire from the heights cut his invading force to bleeding slivers.

With darkness, it was clear that the Confederates had prevailed. And now, too, the night sky above Fredericksburg suddenly lit up with an "aurora borealis" that sent glimmering rays of pure incandescence over the heads of the weary troops. A cosmic light show ... and it was fully matched by the soaring, blazing spirits of the men in gray. For the Southerners had suffered only 5,309 casualties—compared to 12,653 for the Feds.

View of Fredericksburg from east bank of the Rappahannock. (O'Sullivan)
(Courtesy Library of Congress)

What followed—the merciless pillaging of a defenseless city by rampaging Federal forces—would leave a blot of shame on the Union Army that would last for generations. First came the destruction, as the crazed Yankee troopers stripped the homes and commercial buildings of their stores, down to the last scrap of usable lumber. Then they set fires everywhere.

Within a few hours, stately old Fredericksburg was a gutted, smoldering shell—a ghastly symbol of the Federal war machine, which made "warring on civilians" a key part of its military strategy.

For General Lee and many of the other Southern commanders, the sacking of Fredericksburg was a sickening example of the key difference between North and South. The North was more centralized and was ruled by moneyed interests and the railroads: it was the kind of world where you might *expect* the army to make war on helpless civilians.

In the agricultural South, however, with its strong code of chivalry and noblesse oblige, such assaults on the helpless citizenry were scrupulously avoided.

It was the difference between two worlds, two ways of life.

A few days later, Lee would issue a congratulatory order thanking his troopers for what had been accomplished there.

"The war is not yet ended," he would write. "The enemy is still numerous and strong, and the country demands of the army a renewal of its heroic efforts in her behalf.

"Nobly has it responded to her call in the past, and she will never appeal in vain to its courage and patriotism.

"The signal manifestations of Divine mercy that have distinguished the eventful and glorious campaign of the year just closing give assurance of hope that, under the guidance of the same Almighty hand, the coming year will be no less fruitful of events that will insure the safety, peace and happiness of our beloved country, and add new lustre to the already imperishable name of the Army of Northern Virginia."

While some historians insist that the highest point of Confederate success in the war occurred between 2nd Manassas and Sharpsburg, others will tell you that it was here—at Fredericksburg and Chancellorsville (which followed only a few months later)—that the Southern campaign reached its apogee.

But the historical record provides only the sketchiest details about another key incident that took place between Fredericksburg and Chancellorsville ... the moment in which Robert E. Lee came down with a "throat infection" that would gradually deepen into the heart disease that took his life in October of 1870.

"For the first time since 1849," Douglas Southall Freeman would write later, "Lee fell ill. He contracted a serious throat infection which settled into what seems to have been a pericarditis. His arm, his chest, and his back were attacked with sharp paroxysms of pain that suggest even the possibility of an angina."

That's the "medical version," at any rate, of the heart ailment that Lee began to develop outside Fredericksburg, during the brutal, snow-lashed winter of 1862–63.

And yet, remembering what had happened to Lee and his family the previous October 20, with the death of his beloved daughter, Annie, another interpretation of Lee's illness seems possible: had the old soldier's heart begun to slowly "break," on the day that he learned the tragic news from North Carolina, and Major Taylor found him weeping in his tent?

(It would be matter of only a few months, remember, from the announcement of Annie's untimely death until Lee's "heart ailment" began in earnest, in the early winter of 1863.)

Indeed, General Lee himself seems to suggest that the illness he caught at Fredericksburg was the beginning of his laboring heart's slow decline into infirmity.

Writing to Annette at Goodwood, seven years later, he would say as much, while describing how his health problems had actually begun soon after he lost his precious Annie.

White House, New Kent Co: Va.
20 May, 1870

My dearest Annette:

Your kind letter of the 24th April has followed me from Savannah to this place & has been most gladly welcomed. It would give me great pleasure to continue my journey to Goodwood but I cannot longer prolong my absence from Lexington. The examinations will begin next week, & I must be there if possible. But I hope to see you all this summer. If you cannot come to Lexington I must go to see you, for you know that I am always desirous of seeing you.

I shall go to Richmond on Monday 23rd & after a consultation with my Drs. will proceed slowly to Lexington. I shall be sure to see you & you know how gladly you will be welcomed by all. Cannot you be present at Commencement, the last of June? 4th Thursday?

My health is much better than when I left Va: & I am quite comfortable again. I do not know that I can ever expect more. My late attack was an aggravation of the disease that I contracted during the war & proceeded from a violent cold that seized me while the Army was before Fredericksburg. I have suffered from it ever since, & it is heightened by my fresh cold.

The sight of you always gives me so much pleasure, that I am sure it would be beneficial to me. Agnes, you are aware, accompanied me South and came with me here, where I have met your Cousin Mary, who took advantage of my absence to visit her GrdSon. Martha Williams is with her, so that with Fitzhugh & Robert we have quite a family gathering. Mary & Mildred are in Lexington under the charge of Custis, & I presume the latter is anxious to be relieved.

I have been so much grieved to hear of dear Ella's sickness. I hope that she is well again. I think the whole of you had better come to the mountains this summer.

Give my love to your father, to your sisters & all the family. I have so much to say that it seems useless to write. All here unite in regards to you & you always possess the love of

Your most affectionate
Cousin

Miss Annette Carter   R.E. Lee [23]

By the middle of February, the skirmishers along the Rappahannock would have received yet another surprise in a war that was full of them: once again, President Lincoln had decided to change field commanders. Now it was Joseph "Fighting Joe" Hooker who had been tapped to direct the campaign against Lee ... and once again, that campaign was aimed at capturing the capital of the Confederacy, Richmond.

For both sides, March was a month of false starts and false alarms; for Lee, it was another month of extraordinary efforts designed to win supplies for his increasingly ragged and underfed troops.

By April, it was becoming glaringly obvious that Hooker was gearing up for a major engagement in Virginia, and Lee quickly decided that the time was right to take him on.

It was typical Robert E. Lee: So what if the bluecoats on the other side of the Rappahannock now numbered 135,000—while his own beleaguered commanders could muster no more than 62,500 able bodies to answer the next bugle call? The odds were simply staggering ... and yet Lee was planning night and day for an *offensive!*

On the morning of May 2, 1863, the General got what he wanted.

For it was then, on the hilly, rolling countryside that surrounded tiny Chancellorsville, that Lee and his most brilliant lieutenant—General Stonewall Jackson—would together craft one of the most astute and masterfully executed victories in the history of modern warfare.

At Chancellorsville, the key tactical step that turned the tide was a "left-flanking movement" of astounding proportions ... a sudden lightning-bolt to the left in which Jackson sent his entire 28,000-man corps crashing into the right side of Hooker's main force ... triggering a massive rout, a wave of retreating blue as far as the eye could see, until the Confederates were strutting victoriously along the Plank Road with victory in their eyes.

As military historians everywhere would eventually conclude, Lee's decision to "split his forces" at the start of the battle was an extraordinary act of generalship—a daring and risky tactic that would leave him with only 14,000 troops under his immediate command ... against a force that was easily five times as large.

With the cool cunning of a Mississippi riverboat gambler, General Lee disguised his front successfully for several crucial hours, so that the Feds never guessed how thin his ranks actually were. Meanwhile, the cool-headed Jackson directed the "flanking maneuver" with such careful precision that it took the bluecoats completely by surprise, and sent thousands of them fleeing in terror from the sudden lightning-bolt that had been unleashed by Stonewall and his valiant crew.

For the Southerners, it was perhaps their finest, their most glorious hour. But the price, the price!

White-faced and frowning, a stunned Lee was told that his great compatriot and fellow-soldier, Stonewall Jackson, had been felled by his own pickets, who'd fired on him by mistake during a moment of confused alarm.

And Jackson, hit three times in the arms, had already lost one of them to amputation, and was weakening by the hour, weakening and sickening. ... Lee knelt in the mud alongside the river; unashamedly, he prayed that the great warrior would be spared. But it was not to be; once again, Divine destiny had spoken, and once again it would have to be obeyed.

Gunned down by this tragic accident on May 2, Jackson would linger for a week before finally succumbing to pneumonia brought on by his wounds. And although the great cavalry general, Jeb Stuart, would fill in admirably for him in the days immediately after the tragedy, the loss of Stonewall could never be made up.

While Jackson lay drifting helplessly toward death, Stuart and Lee would join their separate units, reforming the Army of Northern Virginia and then turning together to drive the Yanks from the field. Chancellorsville would be remembered as a great Southern victory, with much of it accomplished after Stuart and Lee combined their forces. But that didn't change the ghastly fact: Perhaps the most beloved symbol of the "fighting spirit" of the Confederacy had been buried on a Virginia hillside.

Lee knew that Chancellorsville had been a great victory—perhaps the only time in the history of warfare that an army outnumbered two-and-a-half to one by a much-better-equipped foe had been able to turn the enemy's flank, and then to send it into a wholesale rout. But with nearly 13,000 casualties (Hooker had lost 17,000, but could afford them) to replace, Lee knew that the handwriting was on the wall. Unless he received foreign help, he would lose this war through sheer attrition of men and material.

The great Virginia general also understood one other deplorable fact: at Chancellorsville, he'd lost not only a brilliant commander, but also a "moral force"—a charismatic figure whose fiery presence had loomed as the very image of the Southern will to fight. How would he fare, in the great battles that were still coming, without the great "Stonewall" at his side?

And where would he find the commanders he needed so badly now—the brilliant, selfless men who would help him build on what had been achieved in the sun-baked mud of Chancellorsville?

Searching about anxiously, he would write General Hood in June: "I ... [believe] that our army would be invincible if it could be properly organized and officered. There never were such men in an army before. They will go anywhere and do anything if properly led.

"But there is the difficulty—proper commanders—where can they be obtained?"

For Lee and the Confederates, Chancellorsville had been a victory with 16,792 casualties for the Union and only 12,764 for the Confederates. But the greatest cost of that great battle would be Jackson's tragic death. And the subsequent vacuum of leadership that it helped to trigger would prove decisive during early July, at a tiny Pennsylvania hamlet that would soon become one of America's most hallowed names.

Gettysburg.

CHAPTER SEVEN

Thunder at Gettysburg

Come, General Pickett, this has been my fight and upon my shoulders rests the blame. The men and officers of your command have written the name of Virginia as high today as it has ever been written before.

Robert E. Lee to Major General George E. Pickett, July 3, 1863, and moments after "Pickett's charge" ended in disaster at the Battle of Gettysburg.

In the weeks that followed the great Southern victory at Chancellorsville, General Lee and his fellow-commanders dared to hope that they could find a way to offset the Union's by-now-enormous advantage in men, supplies and transportation. What bold step, what cunning strategy might strengthen Lee's shrinking, half-starved Army of Northern Virginia, before simple attrition and woefully inadequate supplies left him unable to compete with the Yankee juggernaut that every day gathered momentum along the Rappahannock?

As always, Lee would find the answer to that question in a single, stirring verb: *Invade!*

Once again, the only way out of the Federal trap seemed to be the most aggressive way—attack Hooker head-on, right at the heart of his strength, by invading Pennsylvania and cutting his east-west communications, while also isolating Philadelphia and Baltimore.

Jefferson Davis agreed fully with him.

During a lengthy series of conferences in the Confederate capital of Richmond (May 14–17), the Southern President agonized over an east-west problem of his own: should he divert some of his Virginia soldiers to the Mississippi, where they could join the fighting around Vicksburg—or leave them with General Lee, for a spear-thrust north of the Mason-Dixon line?

In the end, Davis opted for the assault on Pennsylvania, and with good reason: as the Northern industrial machine continued to vastly out-perform the South's dwindling manufacturing facilities, Southern hopes more and more depended on the disgruntled "peace party" of the North.

Somehow, Lee and his aides had to find a way to bring the war "home" to the Yankees, and to make them feel its sting. Only then might the growing disgust with the struggle in the North become so pronounced and visible that Lincoln and the generals would feel compelled to accept a political compromise ... a compromise that would surely grant the South the independence for which she hungered so fiercely.

But there was another reason why an attack against Harrisburg— a major railroad junction and commercial center of south-central Pennsylvania, located about 100 miles north of the Potomac—made good tactical sense. Increasingly, Lee's stomach-growling army was unable to find the food it needed in the blasted, war-scorched farmlands along the Rappahannock.

It was a terrible fact, but there it was: if the Army of Northern Virginia intended to continue feeding itself, it would have to abandon the line of earthworks and gun-emplacements along the Rappahannock and run north, lean as some ravenous greyhound, toward the ripe summer orchards and the swelling cornfields of tranquil Pennsylvania.

On the second of June, a weary messenger handed General Lee a telegram: there was no longer any doubt that several major Federal units were pulling out of their encampments along the James River around Yorktown; apparently, the always present threat to Richmond's safety was now lifting a bit.

The following day, Lee began to move parts of his great army westward, toward Culpeper. From there, major elements were to swing north and west, rapidly crossing the Potomac into Maryland, where the arduous trek to Hagerstown and then Harrisburg would begin in earnest. And by the 17th of June, Lee himself would be on the road with his hard-slogging troops, grinding it out mile after mile and day after day, as the great dust cloud of an army on the march rolled northwest toward Shepherdstown and Williamsport, the two major Potomac crossing-points into Maryland.

Interestingly enough, however, there is some tantalizing new historical evidence to suggest that before the Confederate main force began its march to the northwest, General Lee may have taken a brief respite from the war—in order to attend the wedding of one of his favorite young cousins, Ella Carter, at the Carters' "Goodwood" mansion in Maryland.

The evidence for this fascinating (if rather remarkable) possibility can be found in a startling letter—never before quoted by historians —in which Ella Carter's niece, Ella Hall, clearly states that Lee attended his cousin's wedding at Goodwood, and perhaps only a few weeks before the decisive Battle of Gettysburg.

Ella Hall was the daughter of Rosalie Eugenia Carter Hall and Francis Magruder Hall. She wrote the following letter years after the fact ... and she is apparently mistaken when she says that the wedding was in "1860 or '61"—since the records in the nearby Prince George's County Courthouse confirm beyond any reasonable doubt that the marriage actually occurred in 1863.

It's an intriguing possibility, to say the least. Did Robert E. Lee put the smoke and the destruction of warfare behind him for a few days, during the first or second week of June, 1863, in order to celebrate that most ancient symbol of new life and new hope: a marriage?

It seems rather doubtful, but there's no doubt that he was especially fond of the delightful Ella Carter, and would have done his best to attend these nuptials, if he could. The General's son, Robert E. Lee, Jr., said in a later book that "Ella had always been a pet and favourite of my father." Ella had been with Mrs. Lee and Agnes in North Carolina, nursing Annie when she died. And in his letters to Annette, he almost always asks about his "sweet Ella." Perhaps each reader will have to decide the question for himself, after scrutinizing what Ella Hall wrote in her letter many years after the war had ended.

Having always been an admirer of that truly great and good man, Gen. Robert E. Lee, I was much interested lately in reading over a history of his life.

My interest was further stimulated when I read of his relationship, friendship and affection for his cousin, who was my grandfather Carter.

It brought forcibly to mind an episode which had taken place at Goodwood, which was my grandfather's home, in June of 1860 or '61.

The occasion was the wedding of my Aunt Ella Carter, for whom I was named. It was a full dress night affair, and as I was only about three or four years old, it was quite a feather in my cap to be allowed to stay up for the ceremony.

Gen. Lee was very devoted to Aunt Ella, who was my mother's favorite sister, and he was the most honored guest at the wedding.

I was gazing with delight at all the surroundings and each guest who entered attracted my notice. Imagine what a thrill it was to see coming toward me this splendid looking man in uniform, and the greater thrill to have him take me in his arms and hold me over for my aunt to kiss, and then to kiss me himself before putting me down.

Wedding of Ella Carter, 1863

It stands out among my childhood memories and can you wonder that I take pride in such a memory?

Ella Hall

Another time while calling on Goodwood, the Carter home, Gen. Lee was riding horseback—mother was in the yard—he reached down and fetched her up in front of him. [24]

If you consider the fact that Ella could hardly have imagined this lengthy, complicated sequence of events—and that the Prince George's County Clerk could hardly have written down the wrong year for such a socially prominent wedding—it seems entirely possible that Robert E. Lee did pause, just before Gettysburg, to lift a champagne toast to the marriage of his beloved Cousin Ella.

If so, he must have set out for Williamsport with a joyful, refreshed heart ... and he must have found the sight of all these armed, marching men even sadder than usual, as he compared the happy, festival air of the Goodwood wedding to these ranks of tattered, dusty men moving silently toward the Potomac, toward the desinty that would claim them all.

But duty called, and once again Robert Lee would not fail to answer that summons.

From Williamsport, Lee would fire off a supremely hopeful message to Jefferson Davis on the 25th of June: "I think I can throw General Hooker's army across the Potomac and draw troops from the South, embarrassing their plan of campaign in a measure, if I can do nothing more."

Soon after handing the letter to a courier, the General was climbing aboard Traveller in order to ford the river and once again set foot on Northern soil. And he was moving with dispatch; by the next morning, he and his staffers were already riding through Hagerstown en route to Chambersburg, Pa., and the battle that lay ahead.

The plan was to advance on Harrisburg, without delay—provided, of course, that General J.E.B. Stuart and his cavalry troopers could complete their reconnaissance of Federal movements in Central Maryland and rejoin him for the advance across Pennsylvania. Lee needed Stuart's "eyes," and needed them badly; almost from the beginning of this war, he had been counting on the valiant Stuart to lash his horses through huge, sweeping passes of the enemy—high-speed sallies in which the flying swordsman gathered priceless intelligence about Union movements throughout the combat zone.

But as the last days of June began to drop from the calendar one by one, still there was no sign of the valiant Stuart. What could have delayed him?

On the afternoon of the 28th, during a lengthy staff meeting, Lee would tell Major General I.R. Trimble that the Southern chances for victory in the collision ahead were actually quite good. "Our army is in good spirits," Trimble would later recall Lee saying, "not over-fatigued, and can be concentrated on any one point in twenty-four hours or less.

"I have not yet heard that the enemy have crossed the Potomac, and am waiting to hear from General Stuart. When they hear where we are, they will make forced marches to interpose their forces between us and Baltimore and Philadelphia. They will come up, probably through Frederick, broken down with hunger and hard marching, strung out on a long line and much demoralized, when they come into Pennsylvania.

"I shall throw an overwhelming force on their advance, crush it, follow up the success, drive one corps back on another, and by successive repulses and advances, create a panic and virtually destroy the army."

So far, so good. But none of these stirring accomplishments could begin … not until Stuart arrived. And without him, how could Lee be sure about the location of the great Federal army that had been encamped—that Lee assumed was *still* encamped—outside Washington? And yet the days passed, and the famed cavalry riders did not appear. …

What could be the trouble? Day after day, as the Army of Northern Virginia tramped back and forth across the sun-whipped cornfields of southern Pennsylvania, furiously foraging and piling up foodstuffs, Lee questioned his scouts and spies: Any sign of the riders? Any word of Stuart yet?

Never before had the valiant commander of horses let the General down. How could Lee read this terrain ... how could he be sure of Hooker's movements, without his "eyes"? How beautifully Jeb's mounted troopers had displayed their skills in the mountain passes of the Blue Ridge, only a few weeks before, as they fought to keep their Union counterparts from breaking through the line of the Confederate march, and picking Lee's infantrymen off one by one!

But where was Stuart now? Lee shook his head, frowned, watched the summer rain slanting into the low, green hills that flanked a little town named Gettysburg. He was here in Pennsylvania at last; he had led this vast throng into the enemy's very heartland—but without Stuart, how could he reconnoitre?

How could he have known, as the last days of June dwindled down, that the Yankee columns were already on the move, had been on the move for almost a week ... or that the frustrated, infuriated Stuart was caught on the eastern side of those columns, and unable to cross them in order to reach the Confederate encampments just across the Mason-Dixon Line?

On the evening of the 28th, there occurred a strange and chilling moment that Lee would never forget. It came around ten o'clock, when one of his aides knocked at the commander's headquarters tent, which had been set up in a small grove of oak trees on the road outside Chambersburg.

Lee looked up from his endless maps, and found Major John W. Fairfax peering into the tent.

Major Fairfax had some disturbing news for his commander; one of Fairfax's spies, a very reliable operative named Harrison, had made an amazing discovery while wandering the roads of Central Maryland: "Sir, General Hooker and his army are on the march, north of the Potomac."

Lee stared at the man. Then his eyes widened, and he struggled to keep his temper. It was as close as this Virginia gentleman would ever come to an outright display of anger. "I do not know what to do," he said to Major Fairfax in an icy voice the latter would never forget. "I cannot hear from General Stuart, the eyes of the army!"

Then, glaring furiously at the hapless Fairfax: "What do you think of Harrison? I have no confidence in any scout, but General Longstreet thinks a lot of Harrison."

When Major Fairfax could add nothing to Harrison's description, Lee sent him away and ordered the scout, himself, to appear at the command post.

Within 60 seconds, Harrison had confirmed the worst: He had, indeed, rubbed shoulders with two corps of infantry at Frederick —before clearly observing an additional two corps of bluecoats at South Mountain, near Hagerstown.

And there was more, much more.

In fact, said Harrison, it was now common knowledge throughout those areas that Fighting Joe Hooker had been replaced as the commander of the Army of the Potomac ... by none other than General George G. Meade, Lee's old friend from West Point and Mexico!

Lee nodded calmly, doing his best to hide his feelings, and then sent the man on his way.

Then he sat down at his table, and tried to think.

Suddenly, the entire plan of action against Harrisburg was in disarray. If the Federals had already reached South Mountain in force, Lee knew he would have to move, and fast: he couldn't afford to let his outmanned troops get backed up against the slopes of the Blue Ridge foothills, where they might be cut to pieces by a superior force. He must get to more open terrain, by hurrying east, by moving his forces toward ... and now his gaze fell to the map at his elbow, where two small towns loomed in the path of his projected eastward flight: Cashtown and Gettysburg.

The next day, the 29th, was wet and windy; all morning, silver-black rainclouds skidded down a leaden sky. General Lee walked back and forth along the road, then suddenly whirled to bark at a group of officers who were following him:

"Tomorrow, gentlemen, we will not move to Harrisburg, as we expected, but will go over to Gettysburg and see what General Meade is after." But he was wary of this new commander, and told his aides to beware: "General Meade will commit no blunder in my front, and if I make one he will make haste to take advantage of it."

The next night, even as they were marching along the road that led to Gettysburg, a courier raced up to tell General Lee that one of General Henry Heth's brigades had gone into the town during the day to forage for shoes for the soldiers. But the town was swarming with Union cavalry, and the sound of the bluecoat infantry's drums could be heard rattling on the outskirts.

They were here!

But where, where was Jeb Stuart?

Stretched out on the ground beside the Gettysburg road, a sleepless Lee watched the pale white moon race between gauzy, surging clouds. Was Stuart's absence an omen? Never before had Lee gone into battle without the iron support of that great Confederate hero.

And what of Stonewall Jackson, whose steadying presence had carried him through a dozen battles! Would Lee's remaining cadre of top officers—the Ewells, the Hoods, the Heths, the Longstreets, the Picketts—actually be able to provide the fiery, larger-than-life leadership, *Jacksons's* leadership, that Lee had always depended on to carry them through the end of the day?

The next afternoon, July 1, Lee arrived on the outskirts of Gettysburg to hear the sound of artillery rumbling in the distance: the great, three-day battle had already begun. And now, as this first day of the largest military showdown in the history of the Western Hemisphere began to unfold in earnest, the news was very good for the Confederates. After attacks by Henry Heth, Jubal Early and R.S. Ewell, the Southerners were making enormous progress, driving the Federals from their entrenched positions in and around Gettysburg, and forcing them to fall back to the ridges on the south and east of town.

Suddenly, Jubal Early owned tiny Gettysburg ... and the streets rang with the raucous chorus of the Rebel Yell!

Almost unable to believe his eyes, Lee urged Traveller to an elevated perch about a half-mile outside town. Quickly, he huddled with his top commanders ... with Hood and Longstreet and Colonel A.L. Long.

Why not seize the moment, he asked each in turn; why not plunge forward this instant, and mount an all-out assault on the ridgeline to which the disorganized and badly demoralized Federals were now clinging ... the elevated area southeast of town that was known as Cemetery Ridge and adjoining Cemetery Hill?

But it was not to be: one by one, the commanders announced that their men were exhausted; the guns were not in the proper configuration; it could not be done before nightfall without taking risks that bordered on the reckless.

And so night fell, and once again, the Confederates failed to capitalize on a clearcut victory. As the events of the next few days would show, the key to the entire battle was Cemetery Ridge—which had come within an hour of falling into Confederate hands on this opening day.

That night, camped out on Seminary Ridge—about a mile west of the huge Federal emplacement along Culp's Hill, Cemetery Hill and Cemetery Ridge—Lee finally received the word he had been waiting for through all these wearying days: Jeb Stuart had at last surfaced. He was nearby, at Carlisle, but he wouldn't be able to join the fight until the next afternoon.

Hour after hour, he studied the maps and analyzed the positions. He would have only 50,000 infantry and 2,000 horses, against a force that was easily double that size. And by the time Stuart arrived with his 7,000 cavalry troopers, they would be footsore and weary from the road.

Lee's response to these grim odds was perfectly in character. "Gentlemen," he announced to his officers as the staff meeting broke up around midnight, "we will attack the enemy as early in the morning as practicable."

When dawn broke on that second morning of battle, the Northern troops were strung out along a three-mile front that included Culp's Hill and Cemetery Ridge, with the Ridge ending in two hills whose names would one day be familiar to schoolboys everywhere: Round Top and Little Round Top.

One mile to the west, the men in gray ate a cold breakfast along Seminary Ridge and waited to attack at first light.

When the light finally rose, Lee could hardly believe his eyes: most of the long ridgeline was empty! The Federals were licking their wounds, doing their best to replace the two corps that had been mauled the day before—and most of the reinforcements were still out on the roads.

It was perfect! All that Lee needed now was a swift assault by Longstreet's veteran foot-soldiers, 30 minutes at most, and the high ground of Cemetery Ridge would be his. But when he looked around for Longstreet's columns, they were nowhere to be found. Once again, a needless delay had arisen ... and by the time the tardy General reached Seminary Ridge, to find a furiously impatient Lee stalking back and forth beneath the oak trees, it would be too late: already, the Federals could be seen hurrying into position along the opposing ridgeline.

A moment later, General Hood thundered up aboard his gasping horse to report that his columns were strung out behind him, on the adjoining roads, and would require an hour, at least, to get into position for the battle. "The enemy is here," snapped the Virginia general, with a wave in the direction of Cemetery Hill, "and if we do not whip him, he will whip us!"

Hood nodded; but Longstreet, standing nearby, began to complain that General Pickett's troopers had not yet joined up with his own force: would these interminable delays balk Lee at every turn?

By 2 p.m., with the opportunity to take the Yankee ridgeline long past, Lee was reduced to hoping that a lightning-thrust along the left side of the Union line might succeed in "turning" the enemy's flank and thus open a gap through which the Confederates could climb the hill. After that, by grappling with the bluecoats at close quarters, it might still be possible to inflict major casualties, and perhaps even trigger a rout.

It almost worked. Led by the heroic battlers from General William Barksdale's Mississippi Brigade, and sustained by a valiant attack up the left side of Cemetery Ridge by General A.R. Wright and his Georgia foot-soldiers, the men in gray managed to smash their way through the Union lines and briefly capture a piece of the ridgeline. But where were the reinforcements? Where was General Carnot Posey's brigade ... where were the Rebs who had fought so bravely for General W.F. Perry?

Delayed, delayed!

In the end, the few Confederates who had managed to slash their way to the top of the ridge were driven back, and the second day of battle ended with the positions essentially unchanged.

And indeed, more than on any other single day at Gettysburg, the failure to seize these golden opportunities (both at dawn and dusk) revealed one of the hidden costs of the accidental death of Stonewall Jackson: because Lee had been forced to reorganize the entire Army of Northern Virginia, the speed and accuracy of communications among these newly created units had deteriorated badly.

Long after the battle had ended, in fact, Lee would come to understand that three crucial factors had been at work throughout the engagement to undermine his every effort:

- First, the unfortunate—and maddening—disappearance of Jeb Stuart and his 7,000 cavalry troopers had deprived Lee of his "eyes," and had left him without a way of conducting reconnaissance throughout the Pennsylvania theater;

- Second, the loss of Stonewall Jackson had required the massive reorganization, with significant losses in efficiency ... while at the same time robbing Lee of the one commander who would have leaped to take Cemetery Ridge, at the instant of command;

- Third, the endless delays by General James Longstreet and his troopers meant that Lee's main force was constantly out of synchronization with outlying units, so that battlefield opportunities were lost again and again through weak coordination of his brigades.

Meanwhile, time was running out.

And who knew this better than Robert E. Lee ... the same Robert E. Lee who had understood from the very beginning of the war that the South could not afford to simply "trade losses" with the vastly superior Northern military machine? If the Confederacy were going to accomplish the "big win" it so desperately needed in order to influence foreign opinion and also the "peace party" of the North, it had to be *now*.

It had to be July 3, 1863: the most decisive single day in the military history of the United States.

The action began early, at dawn, with a blistering Confederate cannonade of Cemetery Ridge and the two Round Tops. And by midmorning, the outlines of the plan of attack were clear: Longstreet, in command of more than 15,000 troops from several units, was to lead a gigantic assault into the very center of the Union line.

But would the over-taxed and inadequately supplied Confederate artillery batteries be able to lay down enough supporting fire to cover the brutal, uphill assault? Deeply alarmed, Longstreet fired off a shaky note to the Chief of Artillery, Col. E.P. Alexander:

If the artillery fire does not have the effect to drive off the enemy or greatly demoralize him, so as to make our effort pretty certain, I would prefer that you should not advise Pickett to make the charge. I shall rely a great deal upon your judgment to determine the matter and shall expect you to let Gen. Pickett know when the moment offers.

Colonel Alexander read the note, thought about it, and then fired a message back: "General, when our fire is at its height, I will advise General Pickett to advance."

At one o'clock, Alexander loosed his cannons; instantly the hills around Gettysburg began to boom and echo with hundreds of screaming shells. It had begun! But who would send the signal to Pickett? What moment was best?

Suddenly, through a hole in the blowing smoke of battle, Col. Alexander saw several Federal batteries departing Cemetery Ridge. Instantly, he dashed off a communique to Pickett: "For God's sake, come quick. The 18 guns have gone. Come quick or my ammunition will not let me support you properly."

At that very instant, in what may have been the most important single moment of the War For Southern Independence, General George Pickett was confronting Longstreet.

"General ... shall I advance?"

Longstreet thought for a moment ... appeared to hesitate ... then slowly nodded his head.

Pickett turned. "I am going to move forward, sir."

A moment later, he was gone.

He galloped, long hair whipping in the wind, three hundred yards back to where the infantrymen waited for their orders.

"Up, men!" he roared, while his sweating horse bucked and plunged. "To your posts!

"Don't forget today that you are from Old Virginia!"

And so it began, a vast and bloody choreography, the staggering death-ballet that would forever after be known as Pickett's Charge.

While Robert E. Lee, aboard Traveller, watched from his post on Seminary Ridge, the gray-clad brigades began to move out of the woods, onto the open ground between the two ridges. For a few hundred yards they moved across that green and glowing sward with the ease of dancers, or figures in a dream. Their battle flags—more than 40 of them—flapped bravely in the bright summer sunshine, and in the distance the pounding drums sent up a rhythm that those who marched that day would never forget.

They had advanced nearly a quarter of a mile, when the first Federal batteries opened up.

And instantly, one fact became clear: Colonel Alexander had gotten it wrong.

The "18 guns" hadn't departed the field. Instead, they'd been joined by at least 30 more, to form a brutal concentration of firepower from the crown of Cemetery Ridge. And now, as unit after unit of the South's proudest warriors stepped into the sunlit clearing that flanked the ripe Peach Orchard and the gently waving field of still-growing wheat, the Yankee guns began to take them apart.

Moving forward with regular, unhurried strides, the musket-carrying graycoats ignored their comrades who had already fallen; ignored their agonized cries for help; seized their fallen standards and resumed the march across the killing ground. And with every step they took, the hopes of the South were falling around them.

Here Texas lay bleeding, arms crushed and dangling, from a Union shell. And here, beneath this stand of wind-tossed peach trees, North Carolina was expiring slowly, as the bright scarlet went soaking into the sand. And here, along the woodplank fence that fronted the Emmitsburg Road, Georgia lay choking her last, chest ripped open by a Yankee musketball—

And still they kept coming, rank upon rank upon rank, over the highway fences and now they were beginning to climb the first slopes of the ridge, with the bluecoats falling back and the air burning, hissing with fiery tongues of flying lead, as Pickett and Pettigrew and Garnett and Armistead whipped them on and on—

Halfway up the hill! Will they somehow make it to the crest? Will the endless delays and mis-steps and false starts of this endlessly frustrated engagement finally be wiped out, canceled in the supreme euphoria of the all-out victory that Lee has so long desired?

Years later, many of them would remember it as a dream: the soot-blackened faces of the Yankee gunners, as they cranked off round after round from behind the bullet-nicked stones of the cemetery wall; the huge, arcing plumes of oily black smoke, as each artillery round went cannoning up into the bright blue sky from the gun-emplacements above their heads; the surreal crackling of the muskets, like fire eating through cellophane, and the grayclads dropping around them one by one ... until at last the remnant had broken through, had actually reached the line of Union barricades at the top of the ridge:

FIX BAYONETS!

In the dream they are vaulting the stone wall, and their bayonets glitter like some fabulous jewelry in the late afternoon sun of Pennsylvania, and their boots are tearing clods of earth from the ground as they gasp and swing their rifle butts and claw frantically at anything wearing the blue uniform of the industrial, smokestack-belching North that they have come to despise. ...

And now South Carolina has fallen, gone down under a blistering swarm of bullets, and Mississippi lies in a pool of spurting arterial blood, and what about Old Virginia, kneeling there under that towering red pine, her heartbeat failing and the light already fading from her eyes?

For a few moments—an eternity, the survivors would insist later —they seemed to grapple with the outcome still in the balance. But they were too few, too few! Where were their comrades, that vast legion of brave-hearted warriors who had stepped forward on Pickett's command? They were down, they were expiring, and the Confederacy was expiring with them ... after Shiloh and Manassas and Fredericksburg and the glories of Chancellorsville, it was all coming down to this single, unchangeable and tragic fact: They were too few!

And now, as far as the eye could see, the gray line began to shatter, began to collapse inward upon itself, and those few soldiers who could do so were already staggering out of the hellish kill-zone into which Pickett had led them ... already, falling and tumbling and rolling, they were retreating back down the slope of Cemetery Ridge.

Lee patted Traveller's neck once or twice, and then he also began to move. Unhurriedly, his face a solemn, expressionless mask, he cantered to the bottom of Seminary Ridge to greet the broken, returning ranks of the finest and bravest soldiers that the South would ever send into battle.

Battle of Gettysburg, July 1–3, 1863. Dead Confederate soldiers in the "slaughter pen" at the foot of Little Round Top. (Gardner)
(Courtesy Library of Congress)

But many would not be returning. Among the countless Confederate dead were valiant soldiers such as Captain William Murray, a heroic figure who had kept his unit driving forward, even when the air around him was seething with killing lead. (Murray, who died at Culp's Hill, would be buried at Gettysburg and then re-interred at West River, Maryland.)

But Murray belonged to the ranks of the dead, now; General Lee could not help him. "General Pickett," he said in a low, steely voice, as he confronted his retreating warriors, "place your division in rear of this hill, and be ready to repel the advance of the enemy, should they follow up their advantage."

Pickett, beside himself with horror and grief, fought to control his voice: "General Lee, I have no division now! Armistead is down, Garnett is down, and Kemper is mortally wounded."

And then a moment later, General C.M. Wilcox rode up to announce that his Alabama brigade had been decimated. "Sir ... sir ..." and for a moment Wilcox was weeping, but Lee would have none of it: "Never mind, General," he said calmly. "All this has been my fault. It is I that have lost this fight, and you must help me out of it the best way you can."

And then later that night, just before issuing the orders that would start the long retreat back to Virginia and the last phase of a war that the South could not have expected to win, he would lean from his horse, so exhausted that he nearly fell.

"General," said a staffer, "this has been a hard day on you."

Lee nodded. "Yes, it has been a sad, sad day for all of us."

Then, dismounting slowly, he would pat Traveller's neck again, while telling them all:

"I never saw troops behave more magnificently than Pickett's division of Virginians did today in that grand charge upon the enemy. And if they had been supported as they were to have been—but for some reason not fully explained to me, were not—we would have held the position and the day would have been ours."

It was the largest battle ever fought in the western world up to that time—a titanic, no-holds-barred showdown in which more than 165,000 men had participated. On both sides the losses were appalling: Lee lost 28,063 either killed or wounded, and General Meade paid for his victory with more than 23,049 casualties (although his force was nearly twice the size of Lee's).

It was also the turning point of the war, at least in terms of resources and terrain; never again would Lee's Army of Northern Virginia be strong enough to invade the North.

And even though General Meade somehow failed to take advantage of his huge victory and allowed Lee's badly mauled units to creep back across the Potomac to safety in Virginia, for Robert E. Lee and the South, the handwriting was now clearly on the wall.

As the long gray lines inched across the great river into the Old Dominion, they faced as brutal and desperate a winter as soldiers have ever endured. But they would fight on. Robert E. Lee would perform his duty, as he always had.

How could he have known that Appomattox was only 21 months away?

CHAPTER EIGHT

One Single Afternoon at Appomattox

Lexington Va: 28 March 1868

My precious Annette:

I write to you in great alarm. I have just heard of Mildred's engagement, & see nothing between you & the same fate. I beg that you will come on here immediately that I may endeavor to protect you from these voracious young men. Your father seems to be powerless in the matter, & looks quietly on the abstraction of all his daughters.

We hear from all quarters of the perfect happiness of Mary & of the absorbing love she has for my Cousin Bier, & now that Mildred has found her Adonis, I tremble for you.

Tell your father that I see no safety for you but with me, & that he must send you up as soon as possible. Do not say as in your last letter that you "do not know when any of us will get to Lexington again." You must come & spend the whole summer, & go with us wherever we go.

I want to get to Goodwood, & to see you all so much, but you know I can go nowhere now. My only hope therefore is for you to come here. Agnes writes that she is going to see you soon. You must return with her you sweet Annette & let me see you again. Traveller & Lucy are both ready for the road & I trust I will have many pleasant rides with you over the mountains.

Your father will want to go to the W. Sulphur this summer & he must leave you here with us. When will Alice go to Annapolis? I am so glad that Mr Bowie was made Governor & was so pleased with his inaugural address. It was in good taste & good temper & expressed true principles.

If the Country is ever restored to proper Republican Gov't: it must be through the several States. They must unite, not only for their protection, but for the destruction of this grand scheme of centralization of power in the hands of one branch of the Govt. to the ruin all others, & the annihilation of the Constitution, the liberty of the people & of the Country.

If the good and true men in each State will lay aside party & selfish interests ... in that Course which reason ... may shew as the only true ... Country to follow, all will ... If they do not, there will soon in my opinion be an end of Republic(anism) on this Continent. I have tr ... to stay here & therefore shall [be] little affected no matter how events turn: but I grieve for posterity, for American principles & American liberty. Our boasted self Govt. is fast becoming the jeer & laughing-stock of the world.

We have had a hard winter in the mountains—this month has been particularly cold & uncomfortable; but the storm which has been raging all the week I believe is now at an end & there is a prospect of the return of the glorious Sun, which will soon make all things bright. Not withstanding the inclement spring, the fields are green, the buds are shooting forth, the violets have appeared, & the songs of the birds are added to the thankfulness of man, that winter has passed.

(But it) has been a quiet winter with us ... daily visits of Custis & ... circle of your Cousin M ... Mildred and myself ... has only been broken ... occasional neighbor & a lost ... in the mountains. Mildred ... the domestic machine in ... motion & is in her usual indomitable condition.

Her admonitions to the students, cadets & professors & young men of Lexington I hope have been duly appreciated, & I am sure she must have been a fountain of comfort to the young mothers & housekeepers who are anxiously studying the best way of rearing their children & administering their households. If they have gained no knowledge, it has not been her fault. She has been somewhat exercised by a mass of feminine flesh in the form of Miss Mary Dixon this current month, but she hopes to be relieved on the 1st of April. I hope so too. All unite with me in much love, but no one loves you Annette so much as your Cousin

R.E. Lee [25]

———————————— • ————————————

Springtime comes slowly to the mountain towns of the Shenandoah. You see it first in the leaves of the tall oaks and red gums and locusts that dot the Blue Ridge hillsides—a touch of pale green here and there, barely visible, like the first strokes of a landscape artist's brush. Then the weeds at roadside begin to pick up some vivid green. Next the hawthorns and loblolly pines deepen in color, begin to take on that rich, darker emerald, as if promising that one day soon, summer will actually be here.

Three years after sitting down with General Grant at Appomattox, Robert E. Lee found himself walking each afternoon through the gently rolling landscape that contained the campus of Washington College, in Lexington, Virginia. How he loved to breathe the fragrance of this clean mountain air, and while strolling beneath the great water oaks that flanked the President's residence, to meditate on the great events that had occupied the last decade of his life!

By the spring of 1868, the college students and the professors and the local townsfolk had grown accustomed to seeing this tall, slender, silver-bearded figure striding along the campus pathways and wandering among the foothills that flanked the town. What was he thinking? What raw emotions were still surging back forth, beneath that always calm, that always dignified demeanor?

It was hard to say. Perhaps it was only in his letters—and especially in his intimate, family correspondence—that Robert E. Lee allowed even a portion of his feelings to show.

On this particular afternoon in late March of 1868, he would pen a letter to his beloved Cousin Annette in Maryland, and would for a moment speak openly about the crimes that had been committed against the South. In the end, it had been what they had feared all along; such continuing tyranny on the part of the "Northern Oligarchy" had been the major reason they'd fought the war in the first place.

(That letter would also contain an important historical reference to Maryland Governor Oden Bowie, who had married Annette's sister, Alice Carter.)

Walking endlessly through the hills above Lexington, the retired General tried to still the painful beating of his ailing heart, as the memories of what had transpired after Gettysburg came flooding back. The agony that they had all endured! He thought of an afternoon during the great, two-day battle of the Wilderness, in early May of 1864, when he had led his 61,000 troopers into a brutal showdown with Grant in the heavily wooded, fog-shrouded labyrinth that lay west of Chancellorsville. ...

All day long, on May 4th, the Confederates had been repulsing one Federal attack after another along the Plank Road that linked Orange and Verdiersville to Chancellorsville. And now, as twilight fell, Lee's exhausted forces were running out of bullets, running out of shells, running out of strength. Where could he find the reinforcements he needed to hold that road—when there *were* no reinforcements, no fresh supplies?

In a flash, Lee had an inspiration: he had found a hundred or so men from the Fifth Alabama Battalion, momentarily freed from their daylong task of guarding Federal prisoners.

Instantly, these still-fresh troopers were rushed into the fray ... where they immediately sent up a ferocious yowl. So impressive was their version of the Rebel Yell, in fact, that the alarmed Yankees began to drop back in several sectors adjoining the Plank Road. And in the end, Lee had managed to hold that road, through sheer trickery, sheer pretense of numbers.

For Lee, it was a perfect symbol of what this war had become. Outmanned every time he took the field, and with his supply lines increasingly blown apart, he would spend the last year of the war doing his best to deploy his ever-thinning resources to best effect.

Now, pacing along the veranda of the President's House at Lexington, he would tick off the names of those heroic last battles, one by one:

THE WILDERNESS: In the vast, tangled forests west of Chancellorsville, Lee and Grant had slugged it out over terrain so thick and wooded that the fighters literally could not see each other half the time. With only 61,000 soldiers against Grant's 122,000, the Southern commander struggled valiantly to prevent Grant from turning his flank. And Lee succeeded.

While wounded soldiers from both sides lay screaming in the flames of innumerable fires, the two giants fought to a draw. Grant's advance was blunted ... but Lee's dwindling army had lost more blood that it could *not* afford to lose.

Still there were more grievous losses to come. Soon after the Wilderness, and closer to Richmond, the valiant Jeb Stuart would be felled in the Battle of Yellow Tavern (May 11), while battling the forces of Yankee General Phil Sheridan. He would not rise again—an appalling loss for Southern leadership and Southern morale.

SPOTSYLVANIA COURT HOUSE: A few days later in May, the two adversaries clashed again—this time near a small, rural settlement, after Grant turned his huge fighting machine toward Richmond. Grant's warriors took an enormous pounding, but the stocky Union general dug in his heels, firing off a telegram to the Yankee command: "I propose to fight it out on this line if it takes all summer!"

COLD HARBOR: On June 3, only a few miles north of the Confederate capital, Grant attempted a foolhardy frontal cavalry charge: more than 5,000 of his riders were erased within ten minutes.

For the Feds, it was only the latest in a long series of losses: more than 50,000 bluecoats had fallen in the past 30 days. Suddenly, it was clear that the price of attempting to march straight into Richmond would be too high. Bloodied, but with endless resources to call on, Grant sidestepped toward Petersburg.

PETERSBURG: In an effort to surprise the cunning Lee, a defensive mastermind who was stinging him with casualties at every turn, Grant turned south and crossed the James River on a huge pontoon bridge.

Now the Federal commander was perfectly positioned for an assault on the major Confederate railroad complex that supplied the Virginia capital. Grant came very close to taking it ... but then, out of the blue, General Beauregard arrived with several thousand troopers to frustrate him once again.

At last, Grant was driven to a grim conclusion: He couldn't take Petersburg without an exhausting siege. Within a day, his men were digging a vast series of trenches around the city, and Lee's forces had begun to do the same.

The two sides settled into an early version of the "trench warfare" that would become a major feature of World War I. The weeks dragged on, with the tedium broken only by a ludicrous Yankee attempt to blow the Confederate line apart with a monster-sized bomb. It failed —and the Union infantry men found themselves trapped deep in the resulting crater, helpless against Confederate fire.

RAID ON WASHINGTON: It was bold, it was gallant, it was glorious. And it was also doomed. But in June of '64, Lee dispatched General Jubal Early to Washington, with one of the most amazing assignments ever given a military commander: attack an enemy five times your size on the streets of his own capital!

Jubal Early followed his orders. Watching from the parapet of a military fort on the outskirts of Washington, President Lincoln became the only American chief executive in history to come under "enemy fire" during wartime.

No matter how Lee analyzed these titanic battles during the last year of the war, the bottom line was always the same: the South simply faced too large and too well supplied an adversary to hope to prevail.

And when the increasingly besieged Southern commander looked at what was happening in the other theaters of the war, the same grim pattern immediately became obvious: from Chattanooga to Atlanta to Nashville, the crushing impact of the North's industrial advantage was everywhere taking hold.

Walking along the Lexington veranda, or pausing to repair the child's swing that hung from the great oak that dominated the grounds of the Presidential home, the old soldier mentally reviewed the last links in the iron chain that had slowly strangled the few remaining hopes of the Confederacy.

STRUGGLE FOR ATLANTA: In the summer of 1864, while Grant and Lee struggled around Richmond and Petersburg, General Sherman led 60,000 Federal troops against Atlanta.

After weeks of bloody duels on the outskirts, the Georgia capital fell on September 1, 1864, and another nail had been driven into the Southern coffin. A major Confederate railroad system had now fallen to the Feds: how much longer could supplies hold out?

THE RAPE OF GEORGIA: With Atlanta burning behind him, General Sherman led his troopers on a savagely destructive march across the heart of the South. Virtually unopposed, the bluecoats burned everything in their path, across a front that stretched 60 nightmarish miles. Hoping to destroy Southern will to fight, the Federals smashed more than $100 million in property, and committed hundreds of atrocities along the way.

To this day, the memory of the crimes that were committed against civilians during Sherman's "march to the sea" has not been erased in Georgia.

By April of 1865, it was over.

All that remained was the inevitable: with the railroads that supplied Richmond in the hands of Ulysses S. Grant, and with the Confederate troops literally starving in their trenches, or wracked with diseases and dying like flies in the frigid rain, Robert E. Lee at last understood that he would have to endure the final agony: surrender.

When the hour finally came, it was almost anticlimactic: with fewer than 25,000 infantry left in the field, and with no ammunition at all for his heavy guns, Lee understood that further resistance would simply waste the lives of his valiant men.

"There is nothing left me to do," he told a weeping aide, "but to go and see General Grant, and I would rather die a thousand deaths."

And then a moment later, with inexpressible sorrow: "I know they will say hard things of us: They will not understand how we were overwhelmed by numbers. But that is not the question. The question is, is it right to surrender this army?

"If it is right, then I will take all the responsibility."

And he did. Quickly he penned a note to the Union general, asking for a meeting in which they might discuss surrender terms.

They met at the home of Major Wilmer McLean, not far from Appomattox Courthouse. Lee climbed down from Traveller and crossed the yard. He mounted a set of wide, wooden steps and entered a hallway. A moment later he was waiting inside the family parlor for Grant to arrive.

Thirty minutes passed. Then General Grant walked into the parlor.

The Union commander was heavily bearded and still mud-spattered from the field. The two men shook hands, then sat at a small table in the center of the room.

Years later, resting on the veranda at Lexington, Lee would remember the lines they spoke with icy clarity. He would remember that Grant had been very polite, very courteous ... even pausing for a personal reminiscence, before they got down to business. "I met you once before, General Lee," said the man in the thick black beard, "while we were serving in Mexico, when you came over from General Scott's headquarters to visit Garland's brigade, to which I then belonged."

Lee nodded slowly, but neither man smiled: the occasion was too heavy for that. "I have always remembered your appearance," concluded General Grant, "and I think I should have recognized you anywhere."

Lee frowned thoughtfully. How far off, how tiny those battles south of the border now seemed! "Yes," he said to Grant after a bit, "I know I met you on that occasion, and I have often thought of it and tried to recollect how you looked, but I have never been able to recall a single feature."

Now it was Grant who nodded, then waited politely for Lee to continue. The Southern commander took a deep breath; the moment was at hand. Then, with his voice calm and under control: "I suppose, General Grant, that the object of our present meeting is fully understood. I asked to see you to ascertain upon what terms you would accept the surrender of my army."

Grant said nothing, at first; instead of speaking, he called for his notebook and his pipe. But before writing anything down, he summarized the main points for General Lee:

"The terms I propose are those stated substantially in my letter of yesterday—that is, the officers and men surrendered to be paroled and disqualified from taking up arms again until properly exchanged, and all arms, ammunition and supplies to be delivered up as captured property."

And Lee answered calmly, the line that would mean the beginning of the end.

"Those are about the conditions I expected would be proposed."

And then a moment later, General Grant was scribbling out what would become one of the most important documents in the history of the United States.

Gen. R.E. Lee,
Comd. CSA
Gen.

In accordance with the substance of my letter to you of the 8th instat I propose to receive the surrender of the Army of N.Va. on the following terms, to-wit:

Rolls of all the officers and men to be made in duplicate, one copy to be given to an officer designated by me, the other to be retained by such officer or officers as you may designate. The officers to give their individual paroles not to take up arms against the Government of the United States until properly exchanged and each company or regimental commander sign a like parole for the men of their command.

The arms, artillery and public property to be parked and stacked and turned over to the officer appointed by me to receive them.

This will not embrace the side arms of the officers, nor their private horses or baggage. This done each officer and man will be allowed to return to their homes not to be disturbed by United States authority so long as they observe their paroles and the laws in force where they may reside.

Very respectfully,
U.S. Grant, Lt. Gl.

Lee studied the words for a long time before announcing "This will have a very happy effect on my army." Still, he was troubled; he had hoped for one additional benefit for his weary, half-starved men.

"There is one thing I would like to mention." he said after a bit. "The cavalrymen and artillerists own their own horses in our army.

Its organization in this respect differs from that of the United States. I would like to understand whether these men will be permitted to retain their horses."

It took Grant only a few mements to perceive the difficulty.

Quickly, he moved to help Lee with it, as best he could. "Well ... I take it that most of the men in [your] ranks are small farmers, and as the country has been so raided by the two armies, it is doubtful whether they will be able to put in a crop to carry themselves and their families through the next winter without the aid of the horses they are now riding, and I will arrange it this way: I will not change the terms as now written, but I will instruct the officers I shall appoint to receive the paroles to let all the men who claim to own a horse or mule take the animals home with them to work their little farms."

Lee nodded, quickly pointing out: "This will have the best possible effect on the men. It will be very gratifying and will do much toward conciliating our people."

After that, only two details remained. First Lee explained that his desperately hungry troops were in need of rations. But when General Grant asked him how many men remained in his army, General Lee's answer spoke volumes about the tragic state of affairs that had overtaken the Army of Northern Virginia during the last few months of the war. "Indeed, I am not able to say.

"My losses in killed and wounded have been exceedingly heavy, and besides, there have been many stragglers and some deserters. All my reports and public papers, and indeed, my own private letters, had to be destroyed on the march to prevent them from falling into the hands of your people. Many companies are entirely without officers and I have not seen any returns for several days; so that I have no means of ascertaining our present strength."

In the end, Grant agreed to send over 25,000 meal rations immediately ... and all that was left was for General Lee to sign his copy of the agreement. He did so, in a clear, firm hand:

Lieut-Gen. U.S. Grant,
Commanding Armies of the United States.

General: I have received your letter of this date containing the terms
of surrender of the Army of Norhtern Virginia as proposed by you. As
they are substantially the same as those expressed in your letter of the 8th
instant, they are accepted. I will proceed to designate the proper officers
to carry the stipulations into effect.

Very respectfully, your obediant servant,
Gen. R.E. Lee

It was 3:45 p.m. on the afternoon of April 9, 1865. At that moment, the War for Southern Independence began to come to an end —although some of the units still in the field would resist the inevitable for a few more weeks, and the last Confederate Army, commanded by General Edmund Kirby Smith, would not officially surrender until May 26.

After signing the surrender document, Lee rose, bowed to those watching the proceedings, and strode out to the porch. He saluted a few Federal officers, then slowly mounted Traveller. General Grant removed his hat respectfully, and General Lee waved his own.

Then he wheeled his faithful mount, and departed to tell his men in gray the news.

The Southern dream of freedom—of the right of each State within the Union to enjoy its own Constitutionally guranteed autonomy—was gone forever. The America of Washington, Jefferson and Light-Horse Harry Lee was no more.

A Lost Cause! If lost, it was false; if true, it is not lost. If the Cause
is lost, the Constitution is lost; the Union defined by it is lost; the
liberty of the States and the people, which they both at first and for
half a century guarded, are lost.

—Henry A. Wise

MEMORIAL DAY
by James Ryder Randall

Noblest of martyrs in a glorious fight!
Ye died to save the cause of Truth and Right.
And though your banner beams no more on high,
Not vainly did it wave or did ye die!

No blood for freedom shed is spent in vain;
It is as fertile as the Summer rain;
And the last tribute of heroic breath
Is always conqueror over Wrong and Death.

The grand procession of avenging years
Has turned to triumph all our bitter tears;
And the cause lost, by battle's stern behest,
Is worn by Justice, and by Heaven blest.

Dark grew the night above our sacred slain,
Who sleeps upon the mountain and the plain;
But darker still the black and binding pall
That whelmed the living in its lurid thrall.

But taught by heroes who had yielded life,
We fainted not, nor faltered in the strife;
With weapons bright, from peaceful Reason won
We cleaved the clouds and gained the golden sun.

And so today the marble shaft may soar
In memory of those who are no more;
The proudest boast of centuries shall be
That they who fell with Jackson rise with Lee!

Robert E. Lee returned to Richmond, where he was welcomed as the great man he was. Always a man of immense dignity, he rejected the many commercial offers that came his way immediately after Appomattox, and chose instead to become the president of Washington College in Lexington. In the fall of 1865, the General moved his family into the bright autumn foliage of the Shenandoah Valley that he so dearly loved.

When General Lee rode onto the campus in early September to assume his presidential duties, Washington College was little more than an elegant name pinned to the map of Virginia's bucolic Rockbridge County. Originally established as the Augusta Academy in 1749, the liberal arts school had later received some of its operating funds from George Washington, himself, in 1796, and had responded by officially naming itself Washington College in 1813.

In 1861, to nobody's surprise, the 100 or so students of the college had joined Stonewall Jackson's army at Winchester, and had then proceeded to rack up many citations for valor during the long war that followed. Meanwhile, the graceful old campus had been ripped to pieces by Yankee marauders. Now the library was in tatters, the science labs were a blasted mess, and half the campus buildings were little more than shattered hulks.

But on September 20, 1865, General Lee led his first Board of Trustees meeting—and promptly announced that Washington College was back in business. And then on October 2, he was inaugurated during quiet, unspectacular ceremonies that perfectly reflected his softspoken dignity.

Soon the old soldier was well launched on his academic rounds. On a typical day, he would arrive at the campus chapel for 8 a.m. services, then begin his administrative chores, which lasted until perhaps two p.m. Later in the afternoon, he would frequently ride Traveller on long rambles through the countryside—a somber, thoughtful figure, sitting tall in the saddle, whose serene countenance showed that he was slowly making his peace with the great struggle that had just concluded.

But make no mistake: this was no "ceremonial" post that General Lee was holding down. He did immense amounts of work, so great were the demands on his leadership during this period of rebuilding an entire college from the ground up. While expanding the small school's curriculum, he sought to introduce new subjects—farm management, construction, and the like—that would have a practical impact on the battered South. While helping to establish new Law and Engineering Schools, he was forever asking: How could he help his countrymen most?

In a letter of 1866, Lee's strong interest in finding new ways to use "higher education" to aid the war-torn, devastated South shines through his words:

"I consider the proper education of [the South's] youth one of the important objects now to be attained, and one from which the greatest benefits may be expected. Nothing will compensate us for the depression of the standard of our moral and intellectual culture, and each state should take the most energetic measures to revive its schools and colleges, and, if possible, to increase the facilities of instruction, and to elevate the standard of living."

Within a year of Lee's arrival, the college was beginning to pull out of its tailspin. The curriculum had been doubled, the faculty had increased threefold, and even the crumbling library had been restored to life. And the same could be said of the General and his small family. Blessedly reunited, they joined him now in quiet, deeply rewarding pastimes: planting roses out back of the President's house: enjoying simple meals together; sitting around a roaring fire in the wintertime. They were immensely grateful to be together again.

Reverently, the old soldier thanked his God for the chance to spend some additional time with some of the best young men of the South —in circumstances that were blessedly free of the horrors of war. But his tranquil days in Lexington were soon interrupted; the nation hadn't finished with him yet.

The ugly historical period known as "Reconstruction" was beginning, and the Radical Republicans of Congress wanted to hear from Robert E. Lee. So he went to Washington for three days in February of 1866. He testified, as requested, but he was eager to hurry home.

Gratefully, prayerfully, he soon took up the graceful routine of an administrator at a college for some of the South's finest young men. And by doing so his reputation continued to grow, not only in the South but throughout the United States.

His home now was along the Blue Ridge ... among the gentle hills and twisting creeks and deep, sunlit hollows that formed his sweet Shenandoah. And it was from here, from the stately old President's House in Lexington, that the 60-year-old Lee would resume one of the most rewarding and satisfying relationships of his entire life: his lifelong friendship with his Carter Cousins at Goodwood.

How much he had missed his "delightful Annette" and his "lovely Ella" and his "fine friend, Cousin Charles" during these endless years of war and turmoil and bloodshed! And how often now, he would "cast longing looks on the hills of Prince George [Maryland, the site of Goodwood]" and remember the glorious times he'd spend with Mildred, and Eugenia, and Alice, and Mary, and Bernard—the high-spirited siblings of Ella and Annette.

And so it resumed: this friendship between Lee and the Carters —between Virginia and Maryland—that had meant so much to the old soldier over the years. Writing to Annette in May of 1866, soon after returning from his Congressional testimony in Washington, Lee would talk eagerly of his desire to visit Goodwood as soon as possible. He would write Annette often and tell her that she could have all the photographs and everything else she pleased. And he would send her and the family signed photographs (CDVs), and also mail off to his sweet Ella one of the hatbands that he had worn during the War.

Lexington Va
18 May 1866

My dearest Annette

I am delighted at the reception of your letter of the 11th. It recalls so many pleasant thoughts, that I am at a loss which first to express. I have been so long anxious to hear of you all at Goodwood, to learn how you were, and to speak of past events, that to satisfy my inquiries your father will have to bring you all to Lexington.

I was so much in hopes that I should have met some of you when I was in Washington. My stay there was too short to communicate with you, & I know that my only prospect of seeing you was to find you there on a visit. I was greatly disappointed that such was not the case, & cast longing looks on the hills of Prince George.

I am sorry that my former letter did not reach you, as you would have known how often I had thought of you, & how much I have wanted to see you. I supposed that so old a P.O. as Queen Anne would never have been abandoned, & addressed you as formerly. When Mildred returns from Cedar Grove, you must come on & see us, & tell me all that has occurred at Goodwood since I was there. You shall then have all the photographs you desire & everything else you please.

Custis & Fitzhugh are both here & so are Agnes and Mildred. Your Aunt Mary is a great invalid, confined to her chair, in which she can roll about the house & yard. She is otherwise well & always cheerful, & the sight of you will cheer us all amazingly.

We have been hoping to see Mrs. Podestad, but she has deferred her visit till June, & I fear will postpone it indefinitely. I hope she delivered all the messages I left for you. Robert is on the Pamunkey, & Fitzhugh will return there next week. He thinks he will not be able to go to Cedar Grove, though the prospect of meeting Mildred may tempt him to depart from his route. Tell her we all want to see her, & wish she would extend her visit here. Say to Mary a visit from her would give us great pleasure too.

Agnes says she never rec'd your letter which she very much regrets. The rails are now so uncertain & my letters so often fail to reach their *destination, that it prevents me from writing to those with whom I wish to communicate, & when I do, from saying what I desire. To enable me therefore to say all I wish, you will have to come to Lexington. Although our residence is small we can always find room for you.*

I desire in July to carry your Aunt to the Alum Springs of Rockbridge: the waters of which are said to be particularly efficacious in chronic diseases: & then to some of the healing Baths: so see if any amelioration of her disease can be effected.

The Alum Springs are about 16 miles distant, & the Rockbridge Baths about 11, though I do not know that the latter are the most favorable for her. Agnes has never recovered from her attack of typhoid fever last Fall, & is still feeble from its effects. Mildred is our chief support, & though inexperienced, is quite an active housekeeper.

You must tell your Papa that I hope he will be able to get to see us this summer, and he must at any rate tell us whether he will come to the mountains of Virginia, for it may be in my power in that Case to visit him. My only pleasure now is solitary rides over the mountains.

I long for the pleasure of seeing you again, Annette, so you must not fail to come.

All united in affectionate love to your father, Eugenia, Alice, Ella & the several sweet ones at Goodwood, & I am ever most affly yours

R.E. Lee

Miss Annette Carter [26]

Even a brief look at the letters Lee wrote during the years immediately after the war is enough to show how much he valued his connection to the "Maryland Cousins"—and his visits to Goodwood. Sadly, however, he soon realized that his happy trips to Upper Marlborough would have to be curtailed for a while: as a former military leader of the Confederacy, the General had been "paroled" after the shooting stopped, and was required by law to remain in Virginia.

In a letter to Charles Carter in July of 1866, the former Southern commander explains why he can't visit Goodwood at present ...

although he remains eager to see his cousins at one of his favorite Virginia vacation spots, "The Rockbridge Baths."

Lexington Va
21 July 1866

My dear Charles

I rec'd this Morn'g a note from my sweet Annette saying that you had not rec'd a reply to your letter. I presume you have ere this, therefore will only repeat in substance what I then said.

I shall return to the Rockbridge Baths on Monday (23rd) with Agnes & Mildred, & will probably remain there till the end of the week (29), unless Mary may determine to go on to the Warm Springs. You will hear at Goshen, should you come, whether we have passed there on the way to the Warm.

Should Mary determine to remain at the Baths, I shall have to return here about the 1st of Aug. I wish I could promise myself the pleasure of going home with you but I Cannot. The terms of my parole confines me to Va; as it is generally understood; & in addition I have a great deal to do, & but little help—Annette says she will not come to see her Uncle. I did not expect to hear that. She is going to Ella's and any where else also, & she knows no one wants to see her as much as I do.

Hoping to see you soon—

I am very truly yours
R.E. Lee

Chas: H. Carter Esq. [27]

It was a melancholy time. The South continued to suffer terribly from the wounds that were the legacy of the war, and everywhere the scars were only beginning to heal.

Walking slowly across the campus, his eyes on the distant Blue Ridge, Robert E. Lee must have felt again the pain of bitter defeat, the awful grief he experienced whenever he allowed himself to contemplate the vast ranks of the Confederate dead. Would time heal these wounds? Would the simple passage of the years bring him the peace and the acceptance he yearned for? Hiking endlessly along the green, vivid mountain paths and snipping the flower bushes behind the Presidential Residence, Lee tried to come to terms with all of it: hadn't he sought to console others, more than once, by pointing out that we are all the children of God's Loving Providence?

His growing religious faith certainly helped. And so did the delightful, continuing friendship he felt for the Maryland Carters— and especially for those two beauties, Ella and Annette! By midsummer of 1868, in fact, with the war more than three years behind him, Lee's spirits were improving to the point that he could send Ella a thoroughly joyful note in which words like "cheerful" and "comfortable" were not out of place.

Lee had settled into his new life as a Virginia gentleman, by then, and this letter from Warm Springs shows how much he was enjoying his native state:

Warm Springs 25 July 1868

My dear Ella,

The day I recd Mrs. Georges message informing me of your having passed by to the White Sulphur: I sat down to write to you, to express the pleasure of anticipation in soon meeting you: but was called off by the various interruptions to which I am subject. Today having recd your letter of the 23rd it will commence a ...

I am delighted to think that I shall see you at the White: hope that you will not become so anxious about Mr. George as you did at Lexington & hurry off before I could get there. Our plan was to have gone to the hot the 1st or 3rd of Aug. and after seeing you, precious child, that you will get perfectly well for it will add so much to my pleasure to find you looking as I love to recollect you.

I trust your father's health is good & that he & Mildred & Annette will have reached the White by the time I get there. I shall not have much time to remain for I must be in Lexington by the first of September as I have much to do and work very slowly.

This is a very pleasant place and I am becoming fond of the baths, although it is rather warm for my taste. I wish you were here with us as I would enjoy it so much the more. The company is cheerful and everything very comfortable. I hope Mary was well when she left you. Custis is at the White House and Robt. had come up to meet him when I last heard. So the three brothers were together.

My pretty daughters ... I am sorry ... Cousin comfortably established for Mildred & I to have gone to the White leaving Agnes to take care of her Mother. But Mildred was taken sick about a week ago having taken cold from some imprudence & I fear will not be well enough for us to leave her for some time. She has a low fever which has reduced her very much, but the Dr. has commenced giving her quinine which I hope will dispell it.

Agnes, whom you may have heard was quite sick in Md. has improved since her return to the mountains, & your Cousin M's general health I think is better since her arrival here. Her rheumatism is about the same, though she is cheerful & tolerably free of pain. She & Agnes send a great deal of love to you and say they hope they will meet you somewhere in the mountains, & if they do not, that you have to come to Lexington.

I hope your stay was in Petersburg though G ... had gone for her. I had written to her to join us, but she seems to be as much in love with L ... as you are with Mr. George and cannot leave him. He says he cannot leave his business; it all stops if he absents himself. Kiss little Alice for me and tell Mr. George that all with me unite in kindest regards to him. I hope his health is as good as when I parted with him last year.

And now my dear little Cousin I must bid you good-bye. Though always anxious to see you, I am more impatient since you have come nearer to me and my expectations increase as my prospects brighten. Write to Annette that she might come on and see her Cousin for I fear Mr. Claggett will take her from me forever.

> *Your affectionate and devoted Cousin*
> *R. E. Lee*

Mrs. Ella George [28]

CHAPTER NINE

Lee At Lexington

Lexington, Va: 15 July '69

Your letter of the 10th, rec'd this Morn'g My Sweetest Annette, has given me the greatest pleasure, & I can do nothing but think of you & wish to see you. You could not have supposed that a letter from you would "not be acceptable" for you must feel sure that I am always anxious to hear from you. Whenever therefore you wish to give me pleasure, you need not be at a loss how to afford it.

I thought you promised to come to the mountains this summer with your father & to pay us a visit. Tell him he ought to visit the White Sulphur Springs & that the waters will not be half as beneficial to him if you are not with him. There is at present in session here the Virginia Teachers Association. As soon as it is adjourned, I must take your poor Cousin Mary to the Rockbridge Baths which I trust may prove a relief to her. After seeing her comfortably located I must go to the White Sulphur Springs to drink its waters for a season.

If I could see you there Annette I should be content. I expect Martha Williams & Mary to join us at the Baths, in which event Agnes & Mildred will accompany me to the W. Sulphur. I would much prefer to go to Goodwood, & if you will not come to the mountains I must go there to see you. But the difficulty is I cannot say when that can be, for I cannot go about as I please as you can, Annette. I am obliged to be here in September & after the session commences it seems impossible for me to get away.

I am very anxious to go to Goodwood again & will do so the first moment I can. But come up to the White this summer with your father. I enjoyed seeing you so much this spring when I was in Baltimore that I have been comforting myself with the prospect of being again with you this summer.

Mary I am sure can spare you for she will be thinking all the time of her Gen'l.

I must now bid you good bye My dear Annette as I am called into the convention which is sitting in the College Chapel just above me.

> *Most truly & affly*
> *your Cousin*
> *R.E. Lee*

Miss Annette Carter [29]

Twilight. This was the best time ... the time of the hoot owl, and the shadows gathering on the lawn, and the first stars winking through the dusk toward his porch window, toward the window that flanked the small, austere sitting room in which Robert E. Lee would spend his final hours, compose his final thoughts.

It was February, 1870, on the campus of Washington College in Lexington. Gazing through the clear glass panes, the great General watched the deep blue twilight advancing along the grass.

How fleet, how swift the passing years! How distant from him now the rumble of the artillery, the bright piping of the Confederate bugles, the cries of the wounded in their ancient anguish. ...

Robert E. Lee on Traveller and Annette Carter on Lucy Long

For several months now, the doctors had been trying to prepare him for the inevitable. Oh, they never spoke directly of his "chances" … or permitted themselves to speculate about the endless coughing and wheezing and chest-pain that had been troubling him for so long. Instead, they used complicated medical terms—fancy words like "pericarditis" and "angina pectoris"—to describe the hardening arteries, the increasingly clogged and rheumatism-afflicted blood vessels that were slowly freezing the General's heart.

But all of them knew it was medical obfuscation, pure and simple; it was merely a game of semantics. And by now, the inevitable outcome loomed quite clearly, quite inescapably: the General might last to Thanksgiving, perhaps even to Christmas. But after that, the doctors all agreed, the ailing gentleman's future was impossible to predict. …

Yes, the doctors had their fancy jargon, their endless Latin terminology to describe the implacable illness that was slowly destroying the General's arteries and crushing his heart.

He thought it strange, however, to recall how the very first stabbing pains of his terminal illness had actually begun in the mud along the Rappahannock, between Fredericksburg and Chancellorsville, back in the autumn of '62. The terrible cold that had seized his chest, soon after receiving that letter from the courier: his daughter Annie was gone!

Beautiful Annie, only 23, and carried off by the typhoid.

Gasping, coughing until it hurt to breathe, the General had felt the knife turning somewhere deep inside. How would he reconcile himself to this loss, this pain? "God has taken the purest and the best, but His will be done."

How he had struggled to believe that!

Pacing along beneath the tumbling, swirling leaves of that distant autumn, he'd stared out across the muddy Rappahannock for hours at a time. Yes, he'd finally "accepted" it … but after Fredericksburg, his heart had never been the same. Wounded! What had that message from North Carolina been, if not a killing blow to his heart?

Ah, well. What could not be altered would have to be endured. He sat there quietly, calmly, listening to the distant hooting of the restless owl. He watched the evening breeze at work in the needles of the mountain pine. Who could say she was not out there—his Annie—breathing her gentle song into this Shenandoah wind?

He sighed, and reached for his pen.

Robert E. Lee had lived for the sake of his duty; now he would die with it. Duty most sublime! It was time to resume his correspondence with this family he loved. Time to begin putting his affairs in order, to begin preparing all of them for the inevitable end.

Smiling now, he peered through the dimming window at the distant Blue Ridge. This valley he cherished so much—these bending oaks and stately sycamores, and the great shadow of the ridgeline gleaming high above them, and all of it fading slowly now, dissolving toward the darkness that would soon take them, as night gathered in the indifferent towns of his beloved Virginia: *Roanoke, Buena Vista, Lynchburg, Lexington, Natural Bridge—*

Smiling again, the elderly gentleman bent over the desk. The Carters of Maryland had been his finest friends! Somewhere in the hills above Lexington, the nightly hoot owl sent up his mournful refrain. *Whooooooo—it! Whooooo—it!* The old soldier frowned, and began to write to his dear friend Annette, at the "Goodwood" mansion in Maryland.

Lexington Va: 22 Feb 1870

My dearest Annette

Your long silence was most agreeably broken by your letter of the 13th Inst: & I was delighted to find that you were alive & well & still in America. I could not find out until I rec'd Gen'l Bier's letter what had become of you, or what you were doing, for I have lost communication with my scouts in Maryland, but fortunately for me the Adjt Gen'l of the State, aware of my being cut off from all intelligence, came to my aid.

You may well say that you reproached yourself for not having written earlier, for you knew how much I wanted to hear from you; but your kind letter has dispelled all my fears concerning you & I am as content as a man can be who cannot see you. I am unable to visit Baltimore this winter or indeed any other place unless I become better than I am now, for I can make no exertion or undertake the fatigue of a journey.

It is that that has retained me at home & prevented my attending the Peabody obsequies. I am glad that your father has all his children around him or near him & I hope that he is enjoying it as I should if they were near me. I am so sorry to hear that Ella is not well. Tell her there is nothing the matter with that little heart of hers, except that it loves overmuch my Cousin George. The Drs. cannot cure her of that. Absence is her best remedy & she had better come to Lexington & bring you with her. Probably if she had visited the mountains last summer, she might have escaped this visitation.

I have seen very wonderful effects produced on a prostrate nervous system by the Rockbridge Baths though like other wonders they are not infallible. Still they are easily reached in the summer & would bring her near us. I therefore recommend them to her.

My expectation of seeing you this winter Annette was based on the hope that you would come to see your poor Uncle & Aunt, or that I could get to Goodwood, not Baltimore.

I want to visit you at Goodwood once more, to see you all & the place too: but I can form no plans for doing so now. Your Aunt Mary speaks of going to the White House in April to see her children & GrdSon but I do not know that she will accomplish it. Her plan is to take the packet boat to Richmond, three days & nights, & to be transferred from the wharf to the cars for the W.H. I tell her that all whom she desires to see can more easily visit her & spare her the pain & fatigue, but you know how difficult it is to eradicate from the mind of anyone who has the Calvert blood; an opinion once formed. So that if she adheres to her wish I will make every arrangement to facilitate its execution. Mildred is now there, having paid her visit to Richmond, Brandon & speaks of going on to Baltimore, when she has been invited by Mifs Belle Duer, with whom she proposed to spend a week or two & then come home.

Agnes wishes to be in Richmond in April to attend the wedding of one of her friends so has postponed her visit till next month.

She has suffered more with neuralgia this winter than usual, but I am glad that she is not confined to the house with it but is able to go out & to partake of the amusements of the place.

We have had a very nice young lady staying with us occasionally during the winter, Mifs Maggie Johnston, daughter of Genl Albert Sidney Johnston, who was killed at Shiloh. ... [30]

Frowning with fatigue, the old soldier laid down his pen.

He needed to rest a bit. Leaning back in his chair, he closed his eyes. The owl hooted twice; the moonlight was already falling through the window-glass to lie in streaks of alabaster along the polished floorboards of his study. Yes, this was the best time. Just let him doze. ...

In many ways, the last year of his life would be the best one. It was true, he felt increasingly ill. Yet he was greatly comforted by the perpetual, loving presence of his wife, Mary Custis Lee, his children and his extended Lee and Carter families, including the "Carter Clan" of Maryland.

In March of 1870, on the advice of his doctors, he would take his last journey ... and fittingly, it would be a journey through the South, to Florida, in search of the warm, moist climate that might heal his tortured lungs. But first he would stop off at Warrenton Springs, in North Carolina, where he would stand for a few moments at the gravesite of his beloved Annie. How unnatural it seemed, for a parent to outlive his own child in this way, and to stand there leaning into the wind, rehearsing for one final time the sorrow that had first visited him in the mud of Fredericksburg.

After his prayers for her had been said, he rode a sleeping car south to Savannah. At every railroad station, improvised bands burst into

Robert E. Lee and Charles Henry Carter at the White Sulphur Springs
(Greenbrier)

stirring martial music, and admiring parents begged the great general to pat the heads of their small sons—many of whom were in fact named after him—while the girls hurled bouquets of flowers at their idol.

(One of the adoring kids who managed to get in close to his hero would be none other than Woodrow Wilson, the future President of the United States.)

Lee hugged the kiddies, and beamed like the Georgia sun ... but his eye kept straying to the lines of weary war veterans—many of them with amputated limbs—who waited at every whistlestop for a glimpse of him.

At Cumberland Island, between Savannah and Florida, he stopped off briefly for another last farewell: he knew it would be his last chance to see "Light-Horse Harry's" final resting place. What a fighter that old Revolutionary War hero had been! And what determination he and his fellow-warriors had displayed in their battle against the tyranny of that colonial, occupying power! Bending quietly to place a few flowers on his father's headstone, Robert E. Lee must surely have reflected on the price that those 1776 patriots had paid for freedom ... the same price that had been required, nearly a century later, of those men in gray who had dreamed of a Second Revolution.

It was a deeply emotional journey—and it was proving to be utterly exhausting. In a letter to Mary Custis, Lee would quip: "I do not think that traveling in this way procures me much quiet and repose."

And it was true: in spite of the hopes of his physicians, his swing through Florida did nothing to improve his health. What was the point of forestalling the inevitable?

Instead of lingering on in Palatka, Fla., he decided to make his slow, painful way back to Lexington. And it would be a grueling, enervating journey home ... with stops in half a dozen locales—including an especially moving sojourn at the Carter homestead, Shirley, on the James River.

Then it was on to White House, where he would visit son Rooney and his other kin until late May.

He seemed to feel a little better, in May and June, but by the beginning of the summer, he was already taking what would be a final turn for the worse. On the first of July, one day after his 39th wedding anniversary, he would set out for Baltimore to be examined by the renowned medical authority, Dr. Thomas Buckler. Lee had begun to feel worse and worse ... and yet he still had the energy—the strength—to worry about the health of his Carter friends. Because he knew that Ella was seriously ill, he tried to arrange special transportation for her to the healing baths at White Sulphur Springs.

Baltimore, Md., 6 July, 1870

My dear Gen'l,

Mrs. Ella George, daughter of Mr. Chas. Henry Carter, has been very sick this past winter & spring & her father in law, Mr. Samuel K. George of this city, wishes to take her in a private car to the W. Sulphur Springs. The B & O RR Comp. will send the car to Gordonsville provided it can be forwarded on the Ches & Ohio RR. Will you be so kind as to notify Mr. George if the arrangement can be made?

I shall leave here tomorrow & therefore cannot receive your answer.

I am very truly,
R.E. Lee

Gen & Mrs. Chirkham [31]

In mid-July of 1870, General Lee would conclude his last visit to Goodwood—this home-away-from-home that had been one of the brightest, warmest places in his life. Years later, R.E. Lee, Jr., would remember that visit in his book about his father, and would quote a letter Lee wrote to Mrs. Lee from Alexandria,: "I arrived here last evening from Goodwood. ... I got your letter at Charles' ... all went well there and on West River."

A few days later, in a letter to Annette Carter, Lee again refers to West River ... a rural community located not far from Annapolis, where Lee's sister (Anne Marshall), who had died in 1864, maintained a home called "Etowah."

During this last, blissful visit, Lee would spend more than a week strolling across the green lawns of the graceful Goodwood, while enjoying the company of Charles Carter and his seven offspring, all of whom had long ago earned a special place in his heart.

Ravensworth, Va: 19 July 1870

My dearest Annette

I was very sorry to part with you all, & must say in all truth that my regret has not in the least diminished since. But I believe the same would have been the case had I remained with you all the summer, which I would have done had I followed my own inclination.

As short as my visit was I enjoyed it very much, & shall always look back upon it with pleasure. It was a great satisfaction to me to see you all again, at your beautiful home, & to witness your happiness.

I wish I knew when I could see the bright picture that is ever rising in my memory. Mildred I presume has returned from her visit to Baltimore. When you hear her account of her journey to Westriver, I fear that you will not regret not having accompanied us. I did not cease to regret it the whole way & I have not become reconciled to it yet. I would have urged it more earnestly but I feared that you would suffer from the heat on your return next day & were already aware how agreeable it would have been to me.

At Annapolis I was conducted to the Governor's house by the Sec'y of State & Mr. Harwood, & very hospitably entertained by his steward.

On leaving there the heat was excessive, & my pains having been revived at night at Alexa. by a fresh cold taken during the day, my feelings were anything but comfortable. I am better today. I reached here this morning, & was delighted to receive your letter. ... [32]

With each passing week, Lee's illness was settling deeper. Yet he still found time for these ancient friendships, and as late as August 14, was talking happily about them in a letter to Mrs. Lee from Hot Springs: "I heard of Charles Carter's passing up the road to the White, and Mildred preceded him a week. Ella, I hear, is much improved."

A few days later, August 20, he writes from the same place to son Fitzhugh: "You must tell Mr. Carter, Ella, etc., how sorry I am not to see them at the White, but I hope they will call at Lexington. I wrote to Ella on my first arrival here, but presume my letter failed to reach her. You did not mention how her health was."

But the end was fast approaching, despite these cheerful notes. On July 30, he penned his last recorded letter to Annette. Speaking, in this eloquent missive, of the death of Ella Carter's son, Archie, the great general reiterates his belief in Heaven —while mourning not for the vanished young man, but for his grieving parents.

Though he remained silent—ever the steadfast warrior, ever the man of duty—he must have known that his own end was near as he wrote "goodbye, you sweet child."

Annette would live for many years after her cousin's death, and would treasure his memory for the rest of her days.

Her beloved cousin Robert E. Lee would die ten weeks after writing these lines.

Lexington VA: 30 July 1870

My Sweetest Annette

I reached here the beginning to the week, found all well & all regretted that you did not return with me. If I was to tell you that the whole of the regrets felt by the household together, did not equal mine at one moment of my journey or since, you must not think that it was owing to their paucity.

But I need tell you nothing on the subject so I will pass on to something else. I had a very pleasant visit to Ravensworth & Mrs. Futzhugh was

much interested in all I had to say about the family at Goodwood, &
seemed hardly to realize that my cousin Charles could assemble around
him such a numerous progeny. I found the Misses Selden here but the
Misses Johnston had left, & that Mildred had taken advantage of my
absence to fill the house with kittens. She is difficult to satisfy on that
subject but when I get my dog trained and firm, I hope to disperse them.

I am glad that Gen. Bier was successful in his mission to Washington
but sorry that I did not see him in Annapolis. I hope that the mother of
"Annette Carter" continues well & that Mildred had finished her prepara-
tions for the W. Sulphur.

I am glad that Ella has carried her children with her & am sorry at the
death of her little Archie. But he had been saved much sorrow & suffering
by his early departure & as far as he is concerned there is nothing to regret. His parents alone call faith my sorrow.

I was obliged to give up my visit to the White House. The weather was
so hot & I was so painful that I thought it better for me to return & keep
all my misery to myself. I am desired by my physicians to try the waters
of the Hot Springs but am very loth to do so.

If I go I shall be very much tempted to run over & see Ella. I hope that
she is feeling the good effects of the mountain air. There are two English
ladies here, the Misses Laird, daughters of the gentleman who built the
Alabama. They are fine specimens of exuberant health & are going to the
W. Sulphur to see the Country & the people of Virginia. They took tea
with us this ev'g & expressed great sympathy with the South & paid many
compliments to her people. I did not intend to write you a letter tonight,
Annette, but took up my pen merely to divert my thoughts from you a
little, but fear I have not succeeded so I will stop.

Goodbye, you sweet child. All send love to you & all with you. Give
mine to your father, Mildred, Mary, Alice & Eugenia. Remember me to
your kind neighbors & believe me always most affectionately & truly
yours

R.E. Lee

Miss Annette Carter [33]

On the 12th of October, 1870, Robert E. Lee passed into history.

He was a quiet, gentle man who placed honor above all else.

After all the years and all the battles … after his bright, eager youth at Stratford and Shirley and later West Point … after his marriage to the faithful Mary Custis and the birth of his own children … after Sharpsburg and Fredericksburg and the valiant courage of Stonewall Jackson at Chancellorsville … after he had lived and worked and moved among the giants of the 19th Century, General Lee died at the foot of his own beloved, autumn-clad Blue Ridge. He died at home, in Virginia, the place he had loved most.

He died as he had lived—as the greatest giant of them all.

His spirit then passed into the vast green spaces of his mighty Shenandoah.

THE LONDON STANDARD—OCTOBER 25, 1870

Few are the generals who have earned, since history began, a greater military reputation. … His own countrymen learned to look up to him with as much confidence and esteem that they ever felt for Washington. … Truer greatness, a loftier nature, a spirit more unselfish, a character purer, more chivalrous, the world has rarely if ever known. … A country which has given birth to men like him, and those who followed him, may look the chivalry of Europe in the face without shame, for the fatherlands of Sidney and Bayard never produced a nobler soldier, gentleman, and Christian than Robert E. Lee.

Robert Edward Lee (1807–1870)

Epilogue

Mary Randolph Custis Lee, wife of Robert E. Lee, died in Lexington in 1873. None of the Lee daughters ever married. Anges died in the same year as her mother. Mildred lived until 1905 and Mary finally passed away in 1918, after traveling for many years in Europe. Robert E. Lee's son Rooney died in 1891, while his brother Custis lived until 1913. The last of the brothers, Rob, would die in 1914.

Charles Henry Carter would die at Goodwood in 1872. His oldest daughter, Rosalie Eugenia, who had married Francis Magruder Hall, died in 1875. Mary Randolph Bier (who was named after Mrs. Robert E. Lee), who had married Frederick George Bier, survived until 1871. Alice Bowie, who married Governor Oden Bowie, died in 1905. Mildred Carter, who never married, died in 1920. And the only Carter son—Bernard Moore Carter—would become a renowned attorney in Baltimore before dying in 1912. His obituary noted that his cousin, Robert E. Lee, Jr., was in attendance.

Ella Carter George, meanwhile, would go on to marry Samuel George and to live in Ellicott City, Maryland for many years, before dying in 1894. She had been General Lee's favorite—"Sweet Ella," as he had so often called her.

At her death a message was inscribed in her family bible: "Bright, beautiful, loving Ella, thou hast gone! The path of the just is as the shining light, which shineth more & more unto the perfect day!"

Annette Carter would not marry until 1880, when she would wed Henry Brogden, who had been imprisoned at Ft. McHenry during the War as a spy. The couple moved to his family home, "Roedown," located in West River, Maryland. Annette died in 1917.

As for "Goodwood": tragically, the majority of the beloved old Carter family estate would burn to the ground in the 1930's. Only a small part of it would survive. The Lee mansion, "Arlington," which had been confiscated by the Federal government during the war, would eventually become part of Arlington National Cemetery. (The U.S. government would later compensate the Lee family for the illegal annexation of their property, however.)

Confederate soldiers William Murray, James McCaleb, and William Frederick Steuart would be buried at Christ Episcopal Church in West River, Anne Arundel County, Maryland located 15 miles from Goodwood.

Built as a memorial to McCaleb and his sister, Christ Church would one day inspire an eloquent history that contains the following phrase:

> *Times were hard and spirits sad in a neighborhood whose*
> *sons had gone off to fight for a cause doomed.*

APPENDIX

General Robert E. Lee, CSA, 1865 (M. Brady). As was the custom in the 19th Century Lee is standing in front of a door so that the sign of the cross would be behind him.

Courtesy Washington and Lee University

Rosalie Eugenia Carter Hall (1832–1875) was the eldest child of Charles Henry and Rosalie Eugenia Carter. She was named for her mother, who was a Calvert and who was named for her mother, Rosalie Eugenia Stier Calvert.

Bernard Moore Carter (1834–1912) was the only surviving son of the Carters. He became a prominent attorney in Baltimore.

Annette Carter Brogden (1840–1917) She did not marry until 1880 when this photograph was taken. Her husband, Henry Brogden, had been imprisioned in Ft. McHenry during the War as a spy.

Ella Carter George (1836–1894), General Lee's favorite. This photograph was taken in Paris, France in her later years. Lee would always write and ask about his "sweet Ella."

Mildred Carter (1839–1920) was the only Carter girl that did not marry. Here she is pictured with two friends at Goodwood.

Alice Carter Bowie (1833–1905) married Oden Bowie, who as a true Marylander was elected governor of Maryland just after the War. This was the first open election since the War began. Maryland showed where it's sympathies lay with the election of the pro-Southern Bowie.

Mary Anna Randolph Custis Lee (Miley)
Courtesy Washington and Lee University

Eleanor Agnes Lee
(1841–1873)
She attended school at
Staunton, Virginia with
her cousin Annette
Carter.
Courtesy Virginia
Historical Society

George Washington
Custis Lee (Miley)
"Custis" (1832–1913)
Custis became President
of Washington College
after his father's death.
Courtesy Washington
and Lee University

Mary Custis Lee
(1835–1918)
She attended school with
Ella Carter and was the
last surviving Lee child.
*Courtesy Virginia
Historical Society*

Mildred Childe Lee
(1846–1905)
She was the yongest
Lee child.
*Courtesy Virginia
Historical Society*

William Henry Fitzhugh
Lee (Miley) "Rooney"
(1837–1891)
Rooney was a calvary
officer for the Confed-
eracy.
*Courtesy Washington
and Lee University*

Robert Edward Lee, Jr.
(Miley) "Rob"
(1843–1914)
Like both his brothers
he served in the Con-
federate army.
*Courtesy Washington
and Lee University*

Henry "Light Horse Harry" Lee (1756–1818) Robert E. Lee's father (and Charles Henry Carter's grandfather) was a hero of the Revolutionary War and close friend of General George Washington.
Courtesy Washington and Lee University

R. E. Lee, 1838 (William E. West) This painting of Lee was completed two years after he signed the "Goodwood" deed and seven years after his marriage to Mary Custis.
Courtesy Washington and Lee University

Miss Minnie Lloyd, Mrs. R. E. Lee, Mrs. Sydney Smith Lee and Mrs. William Henry Fitzhugh (owner of "Ravensworth")
Courtesy Washington and Lee University

The Carter Bowl

William IV sterling punch bowl, made by Robert Herrell III in London in 1835. Carter crest engraved on front. Storr—Mortimer, London on base.

Hatband and cartes de viste given to Ella Carter George by General
Robert E. Lee after the war. Framed by Bendann's, Baltimore, Maryland.

Robert Edward Lee, 1868 or 1869. (Boude & Miley) At this time General Lee was the President of Washington College (later Washington and Lee University). He would die in October 1870.

Courtesy Washington and Lee University

Descendants of Hon. Charles Carter

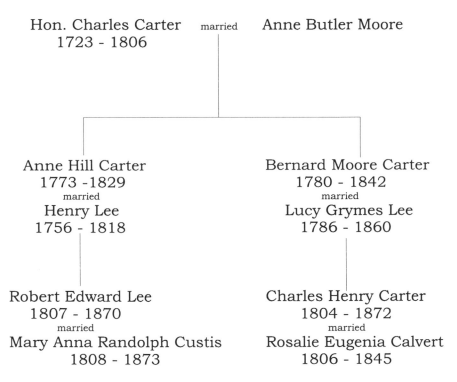

Hon. Charles Carter   married   Anne Butler Moore
1723 - 1806

Anne Hill Carter   Bernard Moore Carter
1773 -1829   1780 - 1842
married   married
Henry Lee   Lucy Grymes Lee
1756 - 1818   1786 - 1860

Robert Edward Lee   Charles Henry Carter
1807 - 1870   1804 - 1872
married   married
Mary Anna Randolph Custis   Rosalie Eugenia Calvert
1808 - 1873   1806 - 1845

Descendants of Benedict Swingate Calvert

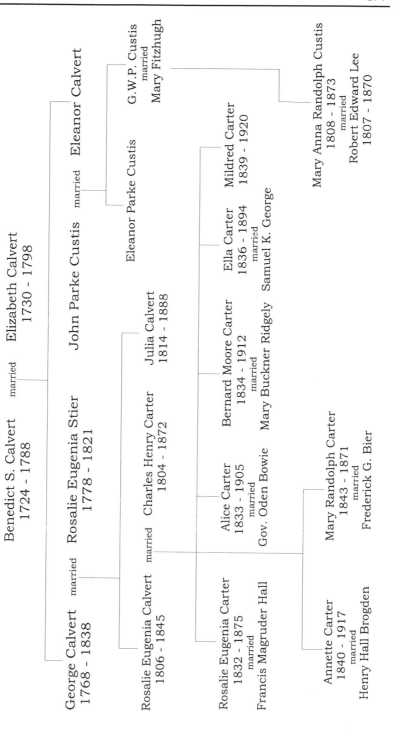

Benedict S. Calvert
1724 - 1788

married

Elizabeth Calvert
1730 - 1798

George Calvert
1768 - 1838

married

Rosalie Eugenia Stier
1778 - 1821

John Parke Custis

married

Eleanor Calvert

Eleanor Parke Custis

G.W.P. Custis
married
Mary Fitzhugh

Rosalie Eugenia Calvert
1806 - 1845

married

Charles Henry Carter
1804 - 1872

Julia Calvert
1814 - 1888

Mary Anna Randolph Custis
1808 - 1873
married
Robert Edward Lee
1807 - 1870

Rosalie Eugenia Carter
1832 - 1875
married
Francis Magruder Hall

Alice Carter
1833 - 1905
married
Gov. Oden Bowie

Bernard Moore Carter
1834 - 1912
married
Mary Buckner Ridgely

Ella Carter
1836 - 1894
married
Samuel K. George

Mildred Carter
1839 - 1920

Annette Carter
1840 - 1917
married
Henry Hall Brogden

Mary Randolph Carter
1843 - 1871
married
Frederick G. Bier

Descendants of Henry "Light-Horse Harry" Lee

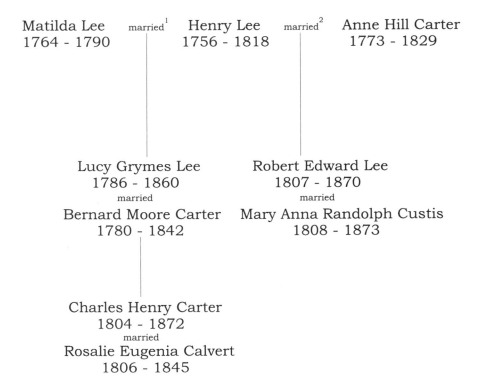

Matilda Lee   married[1]   Henry Lee   married[2]   Anne Hill Carter
1764 - 1790   1756 - 1818   1773 - 1829

Lucy Grymes Lee   Robert Edward Lee
1786 - 1860   1807 - 1870
married   married
Bernard Moore Carter   Mary Anna Randolph Custis
1780 - 1842   1808 - 1873

Charles Henry Carter
1804 - 1872
married
Rosalie Eugenia Calvert
1806 - 1845

ENDNOTES

1) Brady, Patricia, *George Washington's Beautiful Nelly*, pg. 147, April 15, 1824

2) Duke University Library, REL to Custis Lee, May 30, 1859

3) Special Collections, James G. Leyburn Library, Washington and Lee University

4) *Ibid.*

5) Douglas Southall Freeman, *R.E. Lee*, page 88, Vol. 1

6) University of Virginia Library, Jan. 4, 1831, REL to Carter Lee

7) Virginia Historical Society

8) *Ibid.*

9) *Ibid.*

10) *Ibid.*

11) William Franklin Chaney

12) deButts, Mary Custis Lee, *Growing Up In The 1850's*, pages 97 and 103

13) Duke University Library, REL to Custis Lee, May 30, 1859

14) Special Collections, James G. Leyburn Library, Washington and Lee University

15) *Ibid.*

16) William Franklin Chaney

17) Special Collections, James G. Leyburn Library, Washington and Lee University

18) Virginia Historical Society

19) Special Collections, James G. Leyburn Library, Washington and Lee University

20) Jan and William Woodyear, Jr.

21) Special Collections, James G. Leyburn Library, Washington and Lee University

22) Virginia Historical Society, Mary Lee and Agnes Lee letters, Oct. & Nov., 1862

23) Special Collections, James G. Leyburn Library, Washington and Lee University

24) Jan and William Woodyear, Jr.

25) Special Collections, James G. Leyburn Library, Washington and Lee University

26) *Ibid.*

27) *Ibid.*

28) Louise Rede Davis

29) Special Collections, James G. Leyburn Library, Washington and Lee University

30) *Ibid.*

31) Anne Lee Davis Sullivan

32) Special Collections, James G. Leyburn Library, Washington and Lee University

33) *Ibid.*

BIBLIOGRAPHY

Brady, Patricia, *George Washington's Beautiful Nelly*, Columbia, S.C., University of South Carolina Press, 1991.

Bowie, Effie Gwynn, *Across the Years in Prince George's County*, Baltimore Genelogical Publishing Co., 1975.

Callcott, Margaret Law, *Mistress of Riversdale*, Baltimore, The Johns Hopkins Press, 1991.

Coulling, Mary P., *The Lee Girls*, Winston-Salem, N.C., John E. Blair, 1987.

deButts, Mary Custis Lee, *Growing Up in the 1850's*, Chapel Hill, N.C. The University of North Carolina Press, 1984.

Dowdey, Clifford, *The Wartime Letters of Robert E. Lee*, New York, Da Capo Press, 1961.

Freeman, Douglas Southall, *R. E. Lee*, New York, Charles Scribner's Sons, 1934.

Gerson, Noel B., *Light-Horse Harry*, New York, Doubleday & Co., Inc. 1966.

Hendrick, Burton J., *The Lees of Virginia*, Boston, Little, Brown, & Co., 1935.

Lattimore, Ralston B., *Lee*, Philadelphia, Eastern National Park & Monument Association, 1964.

Lee, Fitzhugh, *General Lee*, New York, D. Appleton and Company, 1895.

Lee, Robert E. Jr., *My Father, General Lee*, Garden City, New York, Doubleday & Company, Inc., 1960.

Nevins, Allen, *The Ordeal of the Union*, New York, 1947.

Poore, Ben: Perley, *Reminiscences of Sixty Years in the National Metropolis*, Philadelphia, P.A., Hubbard Bros., 1886

Page, Thomas Nelson, *Robert E. Lee, The Southerner*, New York, Charles Scribner's Sons, 1908.

Randall, James Ryder, *Maryland My Maryland and Other Poems*, Baltimore, John Murphy Company, 1908.

Royster, Charles, *Light-Horse Harry Lee*, New York, Alfred A. Knopf, 1981.

Talbert, Bart Rhett, *Maryland, The South's First Casualty*, Berryville, VA., Rockbridge Publishing Co., 1995.

Thomas, Emory M., *Robert E. Lee, A Biography*, New York, W. W. Norton & Co. 1995.

Primary Printed Materials

Duke University Library, Durham, North Carolina

Enoch Pratt Free Library, Baltimore, Maryland

Greenbrier Hotel, White Sulphur Springs, West Virginia

Library of Congress, Washington, D.C.

Maryland State Archives, Annapolis, Maryland

Maryland Historical Society, Baltimore, Maryland

Tudor Place, Washington, D.C.

Riversdale, Riverdale, Maryland

University of Virginia Library, Charlottesville, Va.

Virginia Historical Society, Richmond, Virginia

Special Collections, James G. Leyburn Library, Washington and Lee University, Lexington, Va.